Isle of Skye

Glenn Heritage

The Horizon Press

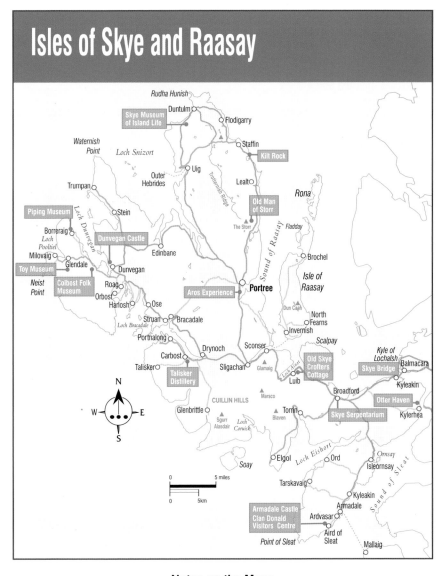

Isles of Skye and Raasay

Rudha Hunish

Duntulm

Skye Museum of Island Life

Flodigarry

Waternish Point

Loch Snizort

Staffin

Kilt Rock

Outer Hebrides

Uig

Lealt

Rona

Trotternish Ridge

Trumpan

Stein

Old Man of Storr

Piping Museum

Borreraig

Loch Dunvegan

Dunvegan Castle

The Storr

Fladday

Loch Pooltiel

Milovaig

Glendale

Edinbane

Sound of Raasay

Brochel

Toy Museum

Dunvegan

Isle of Raasay

Neist Point

Colbost Folk Museum

Roag

Orbost

Harlosh

Ose

Aros Experience

Portree

Dun Caan

Struan

Bracadale

North Fearns

Loch Bracadale

Portnalong

Invernish

Scalpay

Drynoch

Sconser

Kyle of Lochalsh

Balmacara

Carbost

Talisker

Sligachan

Glamaig

Loch Ainort

Old Skye Crofters Cottage

Skye Bridge

Talisker Distillery

Luib

Kyleakin

Broadford

Marsco

Otter Haven

CUILLIN HILLS

Glenbrittle

Tornn

Blaven

Skye Serpentarium

Kylerhea

Sgurr Alasdair

Loch Coruisk

N

W E

S

Soay

Elgol

Loch Eishort

Ord

Ornsay

Isleornsay

Sound of Sleat

Tarskavaig

0   5 miles

0   5km

Kyleakin

Armadale

Armadale Castle Clan Donald Visitors Centre

Ardvasar

Aird of Sleat

Point of Sleat

Mallaig

Notes on the Maps

The maps drawn for each chapter, whilst comprehensive, are not intended to be used as route maps, but rather to locate the main towns, villages and points of interest. For exploration, visitors are recommended to use the 1:50,000 (approximately $1\frac{1}{4}$ inch to the mile) Ordnance Survey 'Landranger' maps. For walking, visitors are recommended to use the 1:25,000 ($2\frac{1}{2}$ inches to 1 mile) Ordnance Survey 'Explorer' and Outdoor Leisure maps.

Opposite: Flora MacDonald's Monument next to the Skye Museum of Island Life, north of Uig

Feature and Walking Boxes

Welcome (Faillte) to the Isle of Skye

Introduction

The Isle of Skye. An enchanting island, known world-wide through the lines of the *Skye Boat Song* and yet an island still with many secrets and surprises for the traveller. Called *Eileann a Cheo* (pronounced ellen a keyo), the Island of Mist, this refers less to the weather than to the air of mystery and romance that surrounds Skye's mountains, lochs, legends and history.

Top Tips

Armadale Castle, Gardens & Museum of the Isles

Boat trips from Elgol to Loch Coruisk

Trumpan Church and walk to Ardmore Point

The village of Stein – many places to visit and pretty beach

Aros Centre – great for families and wet-weather days

Duntulm Castle and the B-road to the Quiraing

Calum's Road, Raasay

Coral Beaches

Dunvegan Castle and Seal Boats

Portree, town, harbour and plenty to do

Stunning scenery with thirteen peaks over 3000ft, numerous waterfalls, soaring cliffs; an enigmatic and colourful history, wildlife abounding and of course, modern Skye, catering for all ages and tastes.

Skye enchants and will richly reward the visitor who takes time and care to learn of the island's history and culture, explore its hidden places and appreciate its grandeur and beauty.

Skye, largely due to the impressive **Cuillin Hills** and the **Old Man of Storr,** is a mecca for climbers; indeed the Cuillin are rated as the best mountain range in the British Isles presenting a serious challenge to climbers. The island is a joy for ramblers and hillwalkers with outstanding views at every turn and some of the most dramatic coastal walks in Britain. It is fascinating for those who love history and archaeology and a wonderland for lovers of wildlife whether marine, birdlife or on land. Children, also, will enjoy Skye and find they can have adventures unique to this island. Both indoors and out families will find plenty to do and new experiences to discover. Our tastebuds are not forgotten either, with Skye boasting several first-class and award-winning restaurants.

Discover the rich **Gaelic** culture and heritage of Skye, home to the first Gaelic medium college at **Sabhal Mor Ostaig**.

Through these pages the visitor is guided along Skye paths, takes in incredible views, explores ancient history, finds wet weather activities and places to visit as well as discovering a way of island life which in many respects exists now as it has done for centuries.

Skye Economy

Principally an agricultural island with much of its income derived from the sale of sheep, cattle and wool. Other income is mainly from tourism with fishing, farm work and the distillery also prominent.

History

Skye was first settled during the Middle Stone Age by Mesolithic hunter-gatherers; remains from 6500BC have been discovered at **An Corran**, near **Staffin**. By 3000BC, Neolithic farmers and herdsmen had arrived leaving chambers and cairns, notably at **Vatten** and **Kensaleyre**. Bronze Age culture probably did not arrive until 2000BC and their legacy is reflected in a change of burial rites using stone slab coffins. These were often placed within cairns from earlier times, **Drinan** and **Kilmarie** are two of very few clues of their time on Skye.

Gradually these cultures merged, and, with the Iron Age settlers spreading north through Europe by 650BC they, too, had settled on Skye building many duns and brochs on the island; that at **Dun Beag** is an excellent example. Elements of all these pre-historic settlers brought strands of their cultures to the island and coalesced into the first native Skyemen emerging as a **Pictish** people who would later surrender much of south Skye to their cousins, Gaelic speaking **Celts** from Ireland. These two branches of Celts witnessed the dawn of Christianity on the island with **St Columba** arriving between 565-585AD. Today, the lovely **Loch Chaluim Chille,** not far from **Kilmuir,** holds remains of the earliest monastic site.

Vikings from Norway began invading and settling on Skye after 794AD. Despite resistance, the Vikings continued to settle and by 1014AD are recorded as fighting side by side with Skyemen to repel Irish invaders. The Norse settlers controlled Skye, led by the 'King of Man' until 1266 when Skye became part of the nation of Scotland joining with the mainland. Estates of the 'Lords of the Isles' were established and the door opened for the rise in power of the clans followed swiftly by clan warfare as each fought the other for control of the island. The MacKinnon stronghold was **Castle Moil**, a gift to their chiefs from Robert the Bruce; the MacLeods, who claimed their ancestry directly from the Norse rulers, held the north from **Dunvegan** whilst the MacDonald's power base in the south was at **Knock Castle**.

Although the MacLeods originally supported the MacDonalds as Lords of the Isles, once the title had been forfeited to the crown in 1493 the battle for supremacy and war between the clans escalated.

Many bloody battles are recorded as well as insults and injustices each to the other which gave rise to vicious reprisal attacks. At **Trumpan** church lie the bones of a great many MacDonalds slaughtered by the MacLeods in reprisal for the MacDonalds burning Trumpan church whilst MacLeods were at prayer one day in 1578. This 'Battle of the Spoiled Dyke' is also a time when the prize possession of the MacLeods, the Fairy Flag, was carried into the battle to ensure a victory. Warfare between the clans continued until 1601 when Skye regained a period of relative peace. During the English civil war many Skyemen died fighting for their clan chief, MacLeod, who supported King Charles I.

Political upheaval in the early eighteenth century gave birth to the 1745 uprising and culminated (from the highlanders' viewpoint) with the Battle of Culloden. At this battle the MacLeods of Dunvegan fought for King George, although the MacLeods of Raasay fought for Bonnie Prince Charlie. After the conflict, in retribution, the Isle of Raasay was ravaged from end to end. **Charles Edward Stewart,** known as Bonnie Prince Charlie, fled, leaving his exhausted highlanders to die or escape, as best they could. For five months he was hidden by loyal followers, moving between mainland Scotland and the Western Isles.

At this point **Flora MacDonald** enters the story, successfully taking him, disguised as a maid, by sea to Skye. One of the best known events in Skye history and immortalised in the *Skye Boat Song*, Flora was arrested for her part in the Bonnie Prince's escape and briefly imprisoned in the Tower of London. Her grave and memorial can be found north of **Uig.** The Prince succeeded in returning to France and never set foot in Scotland again.

After Culloden, harsh reprisals were placed on a crushed and beaten people. Highland dress was banned and arms could not be carried. With the clan

Suisnish and Boreraig Clearances

These neighbouring communities lived out their hard lives for generations until, in 1852 the factor for Lord MacDonald began evictions or 'clearances'. Many families were forcibly evicted in the first round of clearances and most were sent to Campbeltown where they were put aboard the ship, *Hercules*, by the Emigration Commissioners; a large number of these unwilling émigrés died from smallpox long before the end of their journey.

The thirty two families still clinging to their crofts at Boreraig and Suisnish begged to be allowed to stay but were forced from their homes in the autumn of 1853 by repeated visits from the factor's men. The crofters and their children hid during these visits, returning to their roofless homes when they could. One visit was made just five days after Christmas when women and children were turned out to huddle against the walls, crying in the falling snow.

Somehow, eighteen people were known to be still surviving at these townships over the winter 1853 – 54 but by the summer they too were finally cleared from their beloved land.

The townships fell silent, the houses in ruins, to make way for sheep. It is easy to visit these places, a long but not difficult walk and at Boreraig the visitor can stand by the central stone with what remains of peoples homes all around; then, it is easy to hear the echoes of children playing and men and women going about their daily lives in the still air of this sad place.

Broadford Hotel, claimed to be the original home of Drambuie. See 'The Prince's Gift' (opposite)

chiefs turning their eye to finance as money became more necessary than the ability to raise an army, the clan system began to break down and with it, the hopes of a proud and loyal people were betrayed.

Given the political and economic events it was not surprising that a number of highlanders decided to take their chances to build a life abroad and a trickle of émigrés left Scottish shores to find a new life. That natural trickle became a forced flood with the 'improvements' which clan chiefs, many becoming little more than landlords, implemented and which grew to be known as the **Highland Clearances.** Eviction notices were served, people were forced from their burning homes and made to make way for sheep. Across the highlands the clearances gained momentum and many were taken to ships lying in the lochs in chains or by force to become New World settlers.

Wherever highlanders went, by choice or by force, they took their language, culture and traditions. The period 1745-1880 was one of immense upheaval, evictions, famine, poverty and starvation. Ultimately thousands of Scots became pioneers in Canada, the United States, Australia and elsewhere. For those who remained the outlook was bleak. At the mercy of landlords, these crofters struggling to retain their small plots of land began to make their voices heard. After the **Battle of the Braes** and the protests in **Glendale**, courageously challenging ridiculously rising rents and evictions, the crofters finally gained the one thing they needed; security of tenure was granted with the *Crofters Holding Act, 1886.*

The Prince's Gift

Whilst hiding on Skye, Bonnie Prince Charlie repaid the hospitality he was shown by the MacKinnons with a gift appreciated by generations since. The Prince left his recipe for his favourite liqueur and that, according to legend, is how Drambuie arrived in the Highlands.

The population of Skye never recovered its former levels after the clearances; around the year 1800 almost 50,000 people called Skye their home. By 1850, and still today, the population is between 10,000-12,500. Crofting is still prevalent although rarely does it sustain a family. Most crofters must supplement their crofting income by other means and, given the nature of work available on the island, many other residents also combine two, sometimes three, jobs. Against those constraints those who do live on Skye know they are living in one of the most beautiful places on earth; it is a hard place to leave.

Archaeology and Geology

Archaeology

Skye holds a great number of important archaeological sites reflecting its fascinating history. Most are very easy to find although a number are not signposted and for this reason the national grid reference number is given for each site; this will enable anyone using an Ordnance Survey map to locate a given site.

Skye, dominated by the massive Cuillin range, holds evidence of the middens and temporary camps of its earliest, Mesolithic, settlers at **Camus Daraich** in Sleat and **An Corran** near Staffin. An Corran dates from 6500BC and Camus Daraich from 7000BC.

The Neolithic people created chambered cairns and stone circles from 2000BC. Examples of chambered cairns can be found at **Kensaleyre,** and **Kilmarie.** No stone circles such as those found on Orkney or Lewis remain but single stones survive at **Uig** and **Kilbride; Kilmarie** has the remains of a stone circle. There are two stones at **Eyre** which, originally with a third, are said to have supported the great cauldron belonging to mythical Fingalian heroes who visited Skye on hunting trips. Kilmarie is also the site of a single stone slab burial 'coffin' using the earlier cairn at its base. Stone slabs used in bronze age burials can also be seen at **Drinan** and **Kensaleyre**.

When the Iron Age settlers built duns and brochs on Skye they did so with enthusiasm leaving the island almost groaning under the wealth of examples. Whilst **Dun Beag** and **Dun Gearymore** are fine examples many others can be easily explored whilst walking or travelling on the island. Also worth visiting are the **souterrain**; many exist on Skye and yet they are an archaeological puzzle. As yet there is no definite agreement to their purpose although important discoveries at **High Pasture Cave**, a souterrain and one of the most

extensive archaeological excavation sites on this island, are helping to broaden our knowledge. Other souterrain are located at **Ullinish** and **Kilvaxter.**

The Picts left fewer clues to their sojourn here but a **Pictish Symbol Stone** exists at **Tote** close to **Skeabost Bridge**. Early Christians arriving after 565AD established a monastic site at **Loch Chaluim Chille** near Kilmuir and another at **Annait** on the Waternish peninsula.

From 794AD until 1266AD the Vikings were supreme on Skye. However, although four centuries of Viking rule has left a great legacy in place names very little else survives from that time in Skye history. Norse is the origin of many names of townships and areas on Skye, as on much of northern, coastal, Scotland.

Clan warfare raged throughout the medieval period and early castles built for defence include **Duntulm, Brochel** on the Isle of Raasay**, Knock,** and **Castle Moil**. Duntulm, Knock and Castle Moil were abandoned by 1690, their evocative ruins stand testament to an age of fierce loyalty within the clans and even fiercer rivalry between them.

Of particular note and visited only infrequently is the serene **St Columba's Isle**, standing peacefully near Skeabost Bridge and from around AD1200 to AD1500 the site of a small 'Cathedral of the Isles'. Today it is a quiet and pretty spot well rewarding investigation of its ruined buildings and the **Knights Tombstone**.

Later history has added less to Skye's archaeological wealth until we see the evidence of the **Clearances** and of industrial efforts in the nineteenth century. Villages cleared of their people stand empty and silent today; ruined buildings which once heard the chatter of family life can be seen at **Lorgill, Suishnish** and **Boreraig** amongst others.

Early industrialisation has also left its mark and interesting areas for us to discover. There are examples at **Suardal Marble Quarry,** and the **Diatomite Works, Lealt**.

With such varied and rich archaeological sites, many in beautiful settings, any visitor would be wise to include at least some during their travels. On Skye you are never very far from the echoes of the past.

Dualchas, Skye and Lochalsh Heritage Service produce an excellent guide to over 70 sites in the area. Telephone 01478 613857 or available from Tourist Information Centres.

Geology

Within a small island just 50 miles long and no more than 25 miles at its widest point, Skye has a complex geology which gives rise to a natural scenery both outstanding in beauty and varied in structure. Skye is irregular in shape and comprises five peninsulas, Sleat, Minginish, Duirinish, Waternish and Trotternish each with its distinctive characteristics.

In the south ancient Lewisian Gneiss laid down over 2,000 million years ago is found exposed on the eastern coast of Sleat whilst further inland there is a wide outcrop of Torridian sandstone overlying the Gneiss. The sandstone is considerably younger dating back some 800 million years. Southern Skye,

largely composed of these rock layers is a lower lying landscape which is generally less than 1,000 ft above sea-level. Its formation results in a more fertile land than the rest of the island and for this reason the Sleat peninsula is known as the '*Garden of Skye*'.

More or less central to Skye lie the Cuillin, often referred to as one mountain range but in fact two very distinct and different formations. To the east the Red Hills (or Red Cuillin) are composed mainly of granite and have a smoother, rounded appearance whilst the Black Cuillin, much more rugged and striking in appearance, are of gabbro, which is very resistant to weathering and erosion. It is for this reason that the Black Cuillin stand so high in stark contrast to the surrounding area; their magnificent ridge with 11 peaks over 3,000ft is unmistakable and visible not only from most parts of Skye but also from the mainland. First created by volcanic activity, later glaciation has carved great corries and rockbasins between the peaks leaving them standing linked by the narrowest arête. These then are not mountains for the novice climber or hillwalker. Skye maintains two mountain rescue posts and a permanent search and rescue dog team year round.

Volcanic activity also gives us the striking landscapes of northern Skye which is mainly composed of thick basalt lava flows built on top of each other to a depth of about 2,000 ft. In the northwest, later erosion affecting different lava flows to different degrees has left unusual flat-topped hills and stepped plateaux. Western sea cliffs soar above the sea with their ancient basalt

13

Natural World

Otter Walk

Take the Kylerhea ferry road (single track with passing places) off the main A87 road from Kyleakin to Broadford. Turn left at the Forestry Commission sign just before the road end and before descending to the Kylerhea settlement. Leave the car park and follow the wide path to the nature reserve. There are lovely views the length of this path and shortly the visitor reaches the otter viewing hide. Often, Forestry Commission staff will be on hand with advice; otters, seals and seabirds frequent the waters of the Kyle but please remember that patience and quiet bring the greatest rewards.

The Captain and the Eagles

Near the pretty village of Stein is Waternish House, once the home of Old Captain MacDonald of Waternish. According to Skye folk, the Captain managed to tame a pair of wild golden eagles. It is said he went hunting with them and if he shot a rabbit they would swoop down and collect it from his hand.

Walk to Neist Point

From the Glendale road, follow the signs to Neist Point where there is a small car park. From here a very good path leads out towards the lighthouse on the headland. This is a popular area as, beside the lovely views and sweeping Duirinish coastline it is one of the better, and by far most accessible, spots on the island to look out for dolphins, basking sharks, minke whale and all manner of birdlife. Golden eagles, buzzards, arctic tern, gull, kittiwake and many others may be seen; binoculars are a must and this is also a gorgeous spot to watch the sun go down.

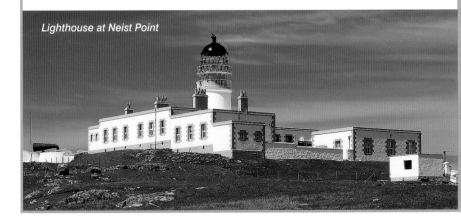
Lighthouse at Neist Point

Castle remains at Duntulm, which was abandoned by 1690

Peat gathering at Loch Leathan, north of Portree

marking clear to see; the highest of these cliffs occur at Dunvegan Head. This northwest corner boasts some of the finest sea-cliff scenery to be found in Britain.

The Trotternish peninsula is dominated by the ridge of the same name and by the Quiraing, high rocky outcrops and pinnacles with odd formations given names reflecting their various shapes. Volcanic activity created the mass of lava flows again lying over each other in waves but in this area the pressures on the underlying rocks were too great and the formations we see today are the result of massive landslips. After the major landslips subsided, weather and erosion combined to leave immense and striking pinnacles such as the Old Man of Storr. The ground here is still moving and rock falls are not uncommon.

Old Man of Storr & Trotternish Ridge

On the northeastern coast the underlying Jurassic rocks are present and this really is the 'Jurassic coast of Skye'. Here, and in parts of central Skye, lie rich hunting grounds for fossils formed 200 million years ago. At that time marine sediments were laid down in rocks which were packed with fossils and to this day discoveries are still being made, showing us further evidence of prehistoric life. Staffin Museum displays dinosaur footprints discovered in Staffin Bay in 2002, some 20 years after the first prints confirming dinosaurs existed on Skye in pre-historic times.

Volcanic activity, glaciation and ancient bedrock, lava flows forming basalt rocks and massive sea-cliffs, and not forgetting the limestone caves such as are found near Torrin and Harlosh; the geology of Skye is indeed complex. It combines to afford the visitor breathtaking beauty and the opportunity to explore and learn more of this ancient island.

John Roberts' book *The Highland Geology Trail* gives a very readable account of the geology of the highlands including Skye.

The Natural World of Skye

'The Isle of Skye – where eagles fly' so reads a popular T-shirt slogan and it is true. There is a possibility of spotting white-tailed or sea eagles, even a golden eagle, from almost any road on Skye. Indeed, Skye is either the permanent residence, or is visited by, over 200 species of bird which makes it a paradise for bird watchers.

In addition to the eagles, who are still very much in need of our protection, the range of species include the corncrake, ptarmigan, skuas, buzzards (often mistaken for eagles by visitors), grebes, swan, osprey, falcon, kittiwake and tern. The list of species is still expanding so great the variety seen on the island. For most visitors it is the chance to spot an eagle that excites and there are a number of places where this may be possible. Many walkers on Ramasaig cliffs or Waternish Head have been rewarded with sightings of sea eagles and they have even been seen from Broadford Bay car park.

Golden eagles, rare and shy of man,

can be more difficult to spot. At home among the crags and mountains the visitor should head for those lonely, rugged spots. Trotternish cliffs and ridge, the Cuillin and Loch Coruisk area are good choices. Not only golden eagles but other birds of prey such as peregrine falcon, kestrels and hen harriers may be seen. Corncrakes can be heard near to Uig and Roag although these birds are shy and rarely seen. Red kite and many others, including the marsh and wading birds, are found around the 450 miles of Skye coastline. Whether bird watcher or interested visitor the best advice must be to make sure you have your binoculars at hand.

Wherever you are on Skye you are unlikely to be far from sighting some special creature. Minke whale, basking sharks and dolphins patrol the coastal waters while by the shores and rocks, otters and seals go about their daily business to the delight of visitors.

Many coastal walks will afford sightings of common seals and sometimes the larger grey or harbour seal. If approached directly by humans, seals will usually head straight for the water where they feel safer, but sit or stand quietly and these lovely creatures will reward your patience. Seals live in colonies and one of the most accessible inhabits the rocky islets and shoreline of Loch Dunvegan.

Otters, too, are naturally resident and could be seen anywhere around the coast. They can be harder to spot in mid-summer when the long light nights give them ample opportunity to hunt late at night when visitors have departed. Otter hides are permanently set up at Kylerhea and on Eilan Ban

where they can be observed without disturbing their daily life. Occasionally they are seen in cottage gardens and on the roads; sadly traffic accidents involving otters are a real threat to their survival. Just two of the many well-known otter habitats are at Rubha Arnish near Broadford and the Staffin Bay coast with the best time to catch sight of otters usually at dusk or dawn.

High cliff walks, particularly Waternish Head, Neist Point and Rubha Hunish on the Trotternish peninsula are the best viewpoints for marine life such as whales and dolphins; of these Neist point is the most easily accessible. Mid-June to early September is the best, but by no means only, time of year for whales and dolphins. Dolphin species include common, Risso's and less frequently, bottlenose and whitebeaked: on a boat trip they will sometimes play alongside the boats. The boat trips from Elgol are particularly good for the range of marine life and birdlife to be seen. The minke whale is the most common of the whales to be sighted and from any clifftop vantage point a calm day without a glaring sun gives the best opportunity to spot whales, dolphins and quite often basking sharks in the seas around the island.

As the visitor walks and explores Skye, perhaps spotting a fox peeking inquisitively through the brush, remember also to look down. Not only the heathers give colour and variety; wild bluebells, violets and primroses as well as the scent of wild herbs and some wild orchids, at various times of the year, show off their vibrant hues and give pleasure to resident and visitor to Skye alike.

Welcome to Sleat – Gaelic bilingual road sign

Highland cattle

Holm Island, near Storr

Once believed to be the 'Land of Perpetual Youth', the Celtic Paradise or Tir-nan-H'Oig this island also held the bones of prehistoric animals and flint weapons which were found by workmen when building the Trotternish road. A view of this island is found by taking the steps from Storr Lochs (signposted on the main Trotternish road) across the road and then keeping to the right as the beach is reached. This is a lovely, peaceful spot and popular with fishermen.

Unspoilt coastal scenery near Duntulm Castle Hotel, on the north-west coast

The Museum of Island Life, north of Kilmuir, Trotternish

The Gaelic Language

Gaelic, often considered a very strange sounding language to non-speakers, is a national language of Scotland and nowhere more evidently so than in the western isles and northern highlands. Even areas further south where Gaelic is rarely spoken today will have predominantly Gaelic origins to their place names.

The Scottish Gealic is a Celtic language related to Breton, Welsh and Cornish and very closely related to Irish and Manx (Isle of Man). Latin writers between 500BC – 500AD referred to speakers of the original language, from which modern Gaelic is descended, as Scoti and to Ireland, their original dwelling place, as Scotia.

Getting to market

Long before the ferry from Armadale to the mainland, and even longer before the Skye Bridge the ancient route off the island was the 'narrows' from Kylerhea to Glenelg.

To take their cattle to mainland markets Skyemen would swim them across these narrows at slack water. Tied nose to tail in strings of 6 or 8 behind small boats up to 8,000 cattle a year were exported in this way. It is unlikely the cattle favoured this method of being transported and yet surprisingly few cattle were lost on these crossings which continued until 1906.

By 600AD Gaelic, spread by immigrating Scoti (Irish Celts) had become established in north west Britain; by 900AD Pictland, as northern Scotland had been known had a new, Gaelic, name; Alba. Although by this time the Scoti (Gaelic speakers) had long referred to themselves as Gaels and on Skye people of Norse origin, Viking settlers, were also Gaelic speakers, the English were well on the way to commonly referring to the northernmost reaches of Britain as Scotland.

Use of Gaelic has declined and risen over the centuries. English dominance from the late sixteenth century made English the language of the law and later, with the *Education Act* of 1872 brought to an end official education in any language but English. Gaelic, although spoken at home in the highlands and the crofts, declined greatly in use with its later twentieth century strongholds resting in the northwest highlands and islands.

The last few decades have seen some revivals in interest and learning; new learners from the cities such as Inverness, Edinburgh and Glasgow and the re-introduction of Gaelic medium schools are doing much to raise again the use of Gaelic as a modern, Scottish language. Skye is home to Sabhal Mor Ostaig, the Gaelic medium college and a number of primary and secondary schools now offer education in Gaelic. There are now many opportunities to learn Gaelic whether young or old and much progress is being made to nurture use of this beautiful language.

Today the visitor will find road signs and town names in English and in Gaelic. If you ask, Skye folk will tell you the meanings of the Gaelic place names;

many derived from natural features and the type of location. Anyone hearing psalm singing in Gaelic at one of the church services on the island will be hearing a sweet, sometimes sorrowful but heavenly sound. It is a language very gentle on the ear to hear but, when written, the constructions of some words appear, at best, tongue twisting. You will often overhear Gaelic being spoken or be welcomed with the word 'faillte' (pronounced felltay) in Gaelic. On another occasion you may hear 'turas math leibh', have a safe journey. Greeting you and wishing you well in their own language is another measure of highland hospitality and Skye has that in abundance.

Food and Drink

The crofting community on Skye produces exceptional fare from a wild and often difficult environment; that they consistently do so on this dramatic land is a credit to the tenacity and success of todays crofters, inheritors of a land which demands to be tended with care and dedication.

As you might expect from an island where you are never more than five miles from the sea, Skye produces a wealth of incredibly fresh seafood, usually the visitor will be eating fish or shellfish in Skye restaurants caught by local fisherman that very day.

In addition, there are a number of family businesses producing fresh, often organic, fruit, vegetables and salads with many delivered to hotels, restaurants and retail outlets through Skye's own FoodLink service which was founded to ensure the freshest supplies from local producers.

Gourmet handmade sausages, venison, hams and bacon are produced on the northwest peninsula as well as poultry. Anyone with a sweet tooth should try some of the puddings, sauces and preserves from Kinloch Lodge; recipes are also available from bookshops and tourist information centres from the pen of Claire MacDonald of Kinloch Lodge. Other islanders produce handmade chocolates, fudges and luxury ice creams.

Supported by Highlands and Islands Enterprise each year the 'Taste of Local Food' awards are made to hotels, restaurants and retailers specialising in using local produce. In September each year some producers take part in 'Gates Open' giving visitors the opportunity to visit and learn about the lifestyle and work of those dedicated to bringing Skye's quality local produce to the market. A farmer's market is held in Portree during the summer months. Aside from a number of retail outlets a number of producers, although not advertising the fact, will welcome visitors who telephone in advance and are happy to give an insight into their work of which they are justly proud.

Skye has its own brewery, situated at Uig, where the range of award winning real ales includes the *Hebridean Gold* a unique beer using porridge oats in its making and very delicious.

Skye has one distillery at Talisker but many who 'know their malts' rate this as among the top three best single malts available. Western Isle whisky is quite different to that distilled on the mainland with a warm peatiness that will convert many to the delight of an after dinner tipple.

Walk to Talisker Bay

For a family with children, the walk to Talisker bay, a pretty sheltered beach overlooked by cliffs and a waterfall, is a good choice. From Carbost, follow the signs to Talisker (not the distillery) and park carefully at the end of the public road by the farm buildings. The way is signposted 'to the beach' and follows an easy, broad path, just over one mile, to the very sheltered bay. There are no facilities but the setting is beautiful and sea-birds can often be spotted over the surrounding cliffs. A lovely way to spend an afternoon.

Talisker Distillery

Skye for the Family

Famous for its mountains and sea-cliffs Skye nevertheless holds many delights for a family and offers beaches which children will love.

Probably the best known is the wide, sandy beach at Glenbrittle with its great views across to the Small Isles. In north-west Skye just a few miles from Dunvegan lies the Coral beach; both are safe beaches for children and there are short and easy walks around which parents and youngsters can enjoy. Only Glenbrittle beach has a shop and facilities.

Some Skye beaches are safe only at, or either side of, low tide. These include Staffin Bay, north of Portree where children can play detective and look for more dinosaur prints; they can also check out those already discovered at nearby Staffin museum. Harrapool and Lower Breakish near Broadford is good fossil hunting ground and at Fiscavaig parents can enjoy peace and quiet while children play amongst the rock pools.

Requiring a sure foot and care so suitable for adults and older children is Camus Mhor Bay, south of Portree, with its two bays and caves to explore.

For rainy days **Skye Serpentarium** at Broadford is a great experience. Home for abandoned and rescued reptiles and amphibians not only are many on view but snake handling sessions also take place regularly. The **Toy Museum** at Glendale is open 7 days a week after Easter and fun for the whole family.

The visitor centres at **Armadale**

Walking on Skye

Where walks are detailed in this book they should pose no difficulty for a person of average fitness and are suitable for children over the age of six and accompanied and supervised by adults. Where a route is referred to, but not described, it holds a level of difficulty which the author deems outside the scope of this book. On any walk, visitors must make their own judgement as neither the author nor publishers can accept any responsibility. It is for the visitor to determine the suitability of any path described taking into account their own capabilities and weather conditions prevailing.

In any event the following basics should always apply:

- Plan any route according to your ability and be honest about your capability and expertise.

- Let someone know where you are going.

- Have a knowledge of basic first aid.

- Ensure you have a local weather forecast.

- Always take the minimum kit with you: strong walking boots, warm windproof clothing, waterproofs, hat and gloves, maps and compass (and the knowledge to use both), whistle, some food and drink, first aid kit, all of which can be carried in a rucksack.

- Remember that the magnetic nature of the Cuillin makes a compass unreliable.

- Know how to call out mountain rescue teams and the nearest route to a telephone.

- Be aware that, in much of Skye, there is no mobile phone (cellphone) network coverage.

- If in any doubt, always turn back.

- Most accidents happen on descent, so take extra care.

- There are numerous apparent paths which in fact are routes following sheep tracks. Whilst useful, sheep have no fear of cliff edges and are extremely surefooted. If the path is heading towards a cliff edge, avoid it and find a safer route.

- Keep children under supervision.

- Respect the environment and follow the access code.

Museum of the Isles and **Aros Centre**, **Portree** were designed with families in mind, so parents and children will find plenty to amuse them when the weather is being unkind.

Outdoors, children are made welcome at Cuillin Trail Riding near Struan, with short rides and tuition available. Skye has a number of boat trip operators and the short seal trips from Dunvegan are a favourite for younger children as well as adults. Other boat trips run from Armadale, Elgol, Portree and Staffin. On Trotternish peninsula **Whitewave Outdoor Centre**, Kilmuir, welcomes families and with fully qualified instructors and guides, its wide range of activities including canoeing, kayaking, archery, windsurfing and guided walks are geared to all ages and abilities. Similarly the outdoor centre on Raasay has a full range of activities for everyone with the ferry trip to the island adding to the experience.

Many walks are suitable for even fairly young children who are often eager to spot whales, dolphins, otters or eagles. Two are given here but there are many others. Armadale Castle grounds have several walks where roe and red deer, otters and possibly even a golden eagle may be spotted.

Finally, always check for town shows, galas and open days or even the Skye Highland Games held early each August. Many areas, including Waternish and Glendale host their own days with games, sheepdog trials and plenty to see and do for the whole family. Visitors should check with the local Tourist Information Centre for information on any local events. Skye has, within a small island, something for everyone.

Arts and Crafts on Skye

A rich seam of talent lies deeply embedded in Skye culture and has produced a variety and scale of arts and crafts on the island which cannot be ignored. Whether due to the inspiring landscape, the sometimes harsh life, or the light and shade which casts enigmatic shadows playing across the glens and mountains Skye has a wealth of talented artists and craftspeople producing such a range that anyone looking for a unique gift or item for their home cannot be disappointed. Wherever you are on Skye there will be studios and galleries close by; the free booklet 'Elements of Excellence' gives details of these and there are a number of 'studio trails' which not only take you away from the main roads through little townships but guide you to discovering the creativity and skill which produces the island's crafts. The visitor should ensure that they do not miss seeing at least some of the studios and workshops, a number of which have won international recognition, and perhaps taking home what can only become a treasured possession from the wonderful array on offer.

Travelling with your dog

Crofting, which is similar to a smallholding, sometimes on a very small scale, is very much part of life on Skye and there are still common grazings where sheep from a number of crofts share open land. Sheep have a habit, apart from not being very bright, of finding their way off their allotted land and on to roads and other open countryside. So although many people do bring dogs with them to Skye it is important to bear in mind that dogs will frighten sheep, may chase them and will be viewed as unwelcome by local crofters. There are a number of areas where dogs are not permitted and others where owners must take responsibility and either keep dogs on a lead or find an area or a walk away from livestock. Never take your dog into a field where there are lambs, calves or other young animals nor into a field of vegetables or fruit. If you are walking a clear path which crosses such a field then keep your dog on a short lead under close control and away from animals.

Cows can be frightened by dogs and may panic or act aggressively. If this happens and cattle move towards you, let your dog off the lead and take the shortest route out of the field with your dog.

When the clock stopped

The Raasay road north from Raasay House passes by the clocktower. It was here that 36 Raasay men assembled to go to war in 1914. As they left the island the clock in the tower stopped never to work again. It resisted numerous attempts at repair to get it working stubbornly refusing to move since that day. Testament, some say, to the fact that only 14 of those 36 men survived the war to return to their island home.

During the bird breeding season, usually April to July, keep your dog under close control or on a short lead in areas such as moorland, forests, grassland, loch shores and seashores to help protect wildlife.

A number of reservoirs and streams are public or private water supplies; if there are intakes nearby keep your dog out of the water. And, finally, never let your dog worry or attack farm animals. For information on walks and safe places to exercise your dog the tourist information centres will have helpful advice.

The Isle of Raasay

Getting there

Raasay is reached by regular ferry service from Sconser on the east coast of Skye. CalMac ferries make up to nine crossings daily on this short trip arriving at Raasay pier which is just fifteen minutes walk from the main village at Inverarish.

The Isle of Raasay, just 14 miles long and 5 miles across at its widest point is, indisputably, a little gem amongst Scotland's Hebridean Islands. With a population of about 200 and the majority of these living in the south, this is an island of beautiful contrasts, which many fail to discover. Raasay can compete with anywhere in terms of its wildlife, history and landscape, and the visitor will be welcomed by its thriving community.

continued on page 36

The Cuillin – Britain's Alps

Without question the Cuillin offer the finest climbing in Britain. The highest peak is Sgurr Alasdair at 3,250ft which may not be high by alpine standards but demands experience, stamina, excellent navigation skills and, particularly, good weather.

Many undertake the world-famous traverse of the Cuillin Ridge, a two day expedition that includes over thirty mountain peaks above sheer mountain corries which rise up straight from sea level.

For anyone who is not confident of their skills across rough terrain and has not ample experience the only way to attempt this traverse is to hire a mountain guide and be prepared for a fairly uncomfortable couple of days. The rewards are coming however, immense and the views stupendous in addition to the unparalleled feeling of achievement.

For many years it was believed that this great range was unclimbable. It was 1836, quite late in mountaineering terms, before the first successful climb of Sgurr nan Gillean and nine years later that Bruch na Frithe was conquered. The climber, Professor James Forbes, also circumnavigated the range and was able to produce the first mapping of the Cuillin.

Another twelve years passed before John Nicol and Algernon Swinburne (the poet) reached the summit of Bla Bheinn in 1857. Two Skye men stand out amongst the early climbers of the Cuillin and these are Alexander Nicloson and John Mackenzie of Sconser. When, in 1873, Alexander Nicolson made an ascent of the highest of the Cuillin peaks it was named Sgurr Alasdair in his honour. Not until 1887 were Sgurr Thearlaich and Sgurr Mhic Choinnich climbed successfully by Charles Pilkington and John Mackenzie; the peaks were named after these two men in their honour.

John Mackenzie continued to make many ascents of the Cuillin peaks during a climbing career spanning fifty years and by 1888 was joined by John Norman Collie with whom he made many ascents and the pair became great friends. Indeed, they are buried next to each other in Sconser.

Still today climbers find new and more difficult routes into the Cuillin and the range still holds many challenges. Perhaps it is for this reason that the famous walking writer, Hamish Brown describes it as 'Mecca – the ultimate.' Certainly the Cuillin remain inspirational and every climber looks to make their own mark on these magnificent hills.

Photographs for this section kindly provided by Tony Hanly of Climbskye mountain guides.

On the In-Pin

Snow climbing in the Cullins

Cioch peak

An evening view from the Cuillins

From Glen Brittle youth hostel there are a number of paths to tempt the visitor towards the Cuillin peaks. For the most part they are well out of the limits of the casual walker. However, for just a taste of this region take the well made path which runs to the south side of a burn by the hostel. Even at the start this path passes a series of waterfalls as the stream tumbles down a small gorge. More waterfalls follow until about one mile on a muddy path to the right is seen. This is quite easy to follow and starts to rise uphill to moorland. As the top of the rise is reached the way ahead is clear. At this point it is recommended, after enjoying the views of Coir' nan Eich and An Diallaid (left) with, to the right, the ridge of Sgurr nan Gobhar, that you make the return trip. Further on the going becomes more difficult and experience, equipment, navigation and energy levels are all required. This route does, however, take you to views that most visitors will not see and in the solitude away from the sometimes crowded Glen Brittle beach the peace and grandeur are all around you.

Whether the visitor does hire a guide and tackle the upper peaks or merely enjoys the views from a distance these mountains never fail to make an impression; visible for miles they are an abiding impression and an integral part of this island.

History and Archaeology

Raasay is a Norse name meaning isle of the red deer. Parts of Raasay's history are still unclear to us but archaeological finds give us clues to the earliest visitors and settlers. Caves in the north of the island have yielded evidence that Mesolithic settlers from Skye crossed to Raasay to hunt and to gather food. It is thought that settlement on Raasay may have begun later than neighbouring Skye possibly around 3000BC. Remains of burial cists and standing stones are evidence of a farming community from about 1500BC and burial cairns can be found at Eyre and Brae.

From the later Iron Age symbol stones such as at Clachan and the well preserved Dun Borodale can be visited.

Christianity is believed to have been brought to Raasay by St Moluag and the earliest cell or chapel erected around 569AD. A later chapel from the thirteenth century was erected over this site and this is referred to as St Moluag's Chapel.

Viking invaders reached Raasay and, as elsewhere, left few clues other than the placenames which are Norse in origin. Following the period of Viking supremacy the history of Raasay is very unclear. Very little is known and it cannot be concluded that the island was continuously settled. Despite this, Raasay has two important monuments from the thirteenth century Castle Brochel and the Chapel of St Moluag.

The mist starts to clear from about four hundred years ago with the times of the clans and the MacLeods of Lewis who became the clan of Raasay. The MacLeods held sway over Raasay for over two hundred years but the island saw some dark days following the Jacobite rebellion of 1745. The Raasay MacLeods had supported Bonnie Prince Charlie at Culloden and later harboured the fleeing Prince as he planned his escape to France. The forces of King George, ensured that Raasay and its people paid the price for loyalty to their Prince and the island was ravaged from north to south.

In the nineteenth century the last MacLeod, in financial difficulty, left for Australia and the new owner wasted no time in clearing the land of its people to make way for sheep. Most of the population, then as now, had lived in the south and a number fled to the north to cling to whatever small but near barren plots of land they could; life was indeed tough for Raasay islanders. In 1919 crofting families were evicted from the tiny neighbouring island of Rona (now uninhabited apart from its caretaker) and eventually allowed to settle on Raasay. Their cottages have been restored and can be seen near North Fearns.

During World War I, Inverarish was used as a prisoner-of-war camp for Germans. Many worked at the iron ore mine which lies, now disused, at the eastern edge of Raasay forest. Others worked on construction and the Burma Road on Raasay gained its name in memory of the German POWs who helped to build it.

Later the twentieth century, brought two Raasay islanders to public attention. The renowned poet Sorley MacLean was born at Oskaig; his poems whether read in Gaelic or English are hauntingly beautiful and tell of an island and a people he dearly loved. His poem *Hallaig* is an elegy to those highlanders who suffered under the clearances.

Bred from necessarily strong and resilient island stock, Calum MacLeod grew up in the north of Raasay at a time when 100 people still lived in the area. As a child he remembered those people asking, and even signing a petition, for a road to their settlement which was served only by a sheep track across the hills. Calum was a crofter, postman and also keeper of Rona lighthouse. By 1964 he and his wife were the only people still living at Arnish in the north. Calum insisted that if a road were built and access to the area improved repopulation would be encouraged.

The Council repeatedly refused and so Calum did what seemed to him the natural solution; slowly and backbreakingly, in addition to his daily work, he took up his shovel, pickaxe and wheelbarrow and began to build his own road. For well over ten years, drawing on undoubtedly great reserves of strength and stamina, he walked the two miles from his house each day clearing and levelling slopes, draining bogs and digging culverts. Calum excavated tree roots with his shovel and his hands, cleared boulders and, eventually completed his road. It still had no tarmac, Calum insisted that was the Council's responsibility. Finally, two years before his death in 1988 the Council were shamed into adopting the road and laying asphalt.

Walk along this road today and it is a walk with spectacular views; it is also a route which, with its creation, one man epitomised the spirit and resolve of a highland people. His simple memorial cairn stands today by the road between Brochel and Arnish that bears his name.

Nature

While south Raasay is low-lying with green and gentle hills, as the visitor travels north the landscape becomes barren and rocky. On the eastern side dramatic sea cliffs rise and are home to Raasay's golden eagles; the west coast is flatter and the land 'flows' to the sea.

Plant life abounds with forty native ferns and a number of orchids growing wild. Wild herbs flourish on the limestone cliffs and in spring the violets, primroses and bluebells wake the island from its winter sleep with a blaze of colour. As the year unfolds heathers, rhododendrons and fuschias are followed by late autumn rowan berries giving the island a unique mix of flora and fauna.

Wildlife includes red deer, from whom the island takes its Norse name, mountain hare and the unique Raasay vole. On the moors golden plovers can be heard and sometimes seen; grouse and woodcock are also present. There are a number of golden eagle pairs who nest on the island and visiting sea eagles. In summer months seals, dolphin, porpoise and basking sharks are present around the coast and numbers of otters are permanently resident along the shores.

Raasay is a small, quiet island yet alive with wildlife, with history and a wonderful place for walkers, photographers and birdwatchers. Dun Caan, the highest point, affords 360 degree views as far as the Outer Hebrides on a clear day. It is home to the Raasay Outdoor centre and provides activities for all ages and abilities. Something for everyone who makes the journey to this lovely isle.

1. South Skye – The Garden of Skye

Armadale and around

If the visitor approaches Skye from the sea by Calmac ferry from Mallaig to **Armadale**, the islands impressive outline, with hills and mountains clearly visible, soon comes into view promising much; the 'Misty Isle' never fails to deliver its promise.

Armadale is a small ferry port and it takes little time to disembark but the visitor should pause here before joining the rush northwards. Many visitors fail to appreciate this southern part of Skye and yet although lower lying than central or northern Skye, there is much to see and do in this area.

Armadale Pier itself is home to a small number of shops which bear investigation including the lovely Ragamuffin, with gorgeous clothes and accessories (open all year), and a pottery. Sea.fari adventures operate from here and, in summer, there is a small restaurant. Outdoor clothes and camping essentials are available from Sleat Trading and there is also a petrol filling station; these are not numerous on the island so the visitor may be wise to refuel here before setting out to explore the island.

South Skye – The Garden of Skye

Portnalong

Carbost

Drynoch

Talisker

Talisker Distillery

Sligachan

Sconser

Scalpay

Glamaig

Loch Ainort

Luib

Old Skye Crofters Cottage

Broadford

CUILLIN HILLS

Marsco

Glenbrittle

Sgurr Alasdair

Loch Coruisk

Blaven

Tortin

Skye Serpentarium

N W E S

Soay

Elgol

Loch Eishort

Ord

Isleornsay

0   5 miles

0   5km

Tarskavaig

Kyleakin

Armadale

Armadale Castle Clan Donald Visitors Centre

Ardvasar

Point of Sleat

Mallaig

If the journey to Skye has been long and time allows then just south from the carpark at Armadale is **Rubha Phoil** Forest Gardens, Walks and Herb Nursery. This is a pretty woodland area with good paths and excellent chances of spotting wildlife including otters by the low-lying coast and seals on the nearby islets.

From Armadale take the single track road south towards Ardvasar and Point of Sleat.

Ardvasar is an attractive township with accommodation and a good grocery shop. The road does narrow even further from here so care is needed until the visitor reaches the tiny township of Aird of Sleat. From the village a walking track runs for 2 miles down to **Point of Sleat**. Along the way the visitor passes a tiny harbour and a cottage before reaching the lighthouse at the Point. This is open, empty land and feels remote with a sense of wide skies and even wider seas giving delightful views of Rhum and Eigg as well as a first glimpse of the Cuillin dominant in the distance.

The seal-maidens of Port na Fagaich

Not far from Ardvasar is tiny Port na Fagaich or the Bay of the Forsaken Ones. Here can be seen a number of large upright stones standing just offshore.

Legend has it that one night a group of fishermen came to the bay and saw something splashing in the moonlit waters. As they crept nearer they realised it was a number of seal-maidens (a little like mermaids) swimming in the seas.

The seal-maidens had taken off their sealskins and their beauty enchanted the fishermen. One of the men stole the sealskins and, when the maidens became distressed at their loss, were comforted by the remaining fishermen on the shore. Each seal-maiden married a fisherman and they lived happily for a year.

At the end of the year, the sea called to the maidens who had no choice but to obey its call and return to the sea. The fishermen entered the sea, trying to hold on to their wives and were turned into the great stones, destined to stand forever near the shore.

Seal-maidens never forget and it is said if you stand at the bay in the soft moonlight you will see each seal-maiden keeping her tryst with her own stone.

Travelling North

Returning by the same route and passing Armadale the road (the A85), soon reaches **Armadale Castle** and the **Clan Donald Visitor Centre**. With the **Museum of the Isles** also within the extensive grounds this is an essential visit. There are many easy walks in the grounds and the Centre, Gardens and ruined Castle represent good value for a day out which will entertain the children. Always check for any events which may be taking place. Here too, is the Clan Donald library which is a resource much used by MacDonalds from all over the world.

A mile further north along the A85, just by the Gaelic medium college of **Sabhal Mhor Ostaig**, itself often a venue for arts and music, is a minor road leading northwest. This route is well worth taking but first, continue north on the main road for a couple of miles to **Knock Bay**, overlooked by the ruinous Knock Castle at the furthest edge of the bay. Built around 1300 and abandoned during the 1600's today it is home to the ghost of the Green Lady kept company by another spirit said to care for cattle in the surrounding area.

Just a few minutes further and the visitor reaches **CamusCross** and **Isleornsay**; turning right here will lead to the very pretty village of Isleornsay. Clustered around one of the best natural harbours of Skye this village of mainly whitewashed houses is a picturesque gem.

Once a thriving herring port, Isleornsay was a stop off point during the 19th century for steamers from Glasgow arriving via the Crinan Canal.

It became a very popular resort and is still dominated by the Isleornsay Hotel. The village also became, in 1820, proud owner of Skye's first public toilets.

This is a beautiful setting; in the foreground is the island of **Ornsay** which is accessible on foot at low tide and, in the distance loom the mountains of the mainland. The *Gallery an Talla Dearg* by the pier with sculptures by Laurence Brodick is worth visiting.

For somewhere different to stay, tucked away from the summer crowds, this is a place well loved by those who have discovered it.

Western solitude

Retracing the route just a few miles brings the road back to the junction where a right turn takes the minor road by the college and leads over hills and wooded valleys towards the western coast. This road is, fortunately, quiet with little traffic since it is a series of small hills, some sharp descents and relatively few passing places. It is a route to be driven slowly and enjoyed as it winds towards **Tarskavaig**.

Just before the crofts, by Gillean, is the large sweeping beach of Tarskavaig Bay with lovely distant views of the **Cuillin** and the headland by **Elgol**.

Further, past the township of Tarskavaig, guarding the tiny bay of Ob Gavscavaig stands the ruins of Dunscaith Castle.

> ## Dunscaith
>
> **Dunscaith** is thought to have been once an immense and impregnable fortress, a stronghold of the MacDonalds of the Isles. The name is said to mean Fort of Gloom. Dunscaith was the home of the fabled Chuchullin, friend to Fingal of Celtic legend (and of the famous cave) and both Skye and Dunscaith feature in the epic poem *Ossian* by MacPherson. According to legend Dunscaith was built in a single day and, after Chuchullin died in battle and his wife, Bragela, died of a broken heart waiting for his return at Dunscaith, the castle fell into ruins in a single night.

Whatever legends may say, and there are many written about Dunscaith, this is a wild and beautiful place with an atmosphere quite apart from other, better known, parts of Skye.

The road from Tarskavaig to **Ord** passes moorland, little lochs, tumbling burns and twisting hills giving views over Dunscaith to the Cuillin and **Blaven** across **Loch Eishort**. Further on the road passes natural woods of oak, hazel and birch; again, rare to Skye where the vast majority of woodland is planted and managed by Forestry Enterprise. This woodland is said to have been a sacred grove of the Druids. There is a timelessness in this unspoilt area and a great sense of the past. By the Ord river is a little hill and on it the ruins of the tiny chapel of St Chaon and its ancient graveyard. Tales abound here of the legendary Fion, of the maiden

The Museum of the Isles

Ord and the road from Tarskavaig on Loch Eishort

Gormhuil who was imprisoned by an evil giant who lived on the Ridge of Ord. You can feel their echoes in this spot.

In 1863 a worker at Ord House, now an hotel, emigrated to New Zealand and sent back home the seeds of the Cabbage Tree, then unknown in Britain. Two of the seeds flourished becoming the only specimens of this native New Zealand palm to successfully grow in the open in Britain. At over twenty feet high and flowering every seventh year they fill the garden at Ord with the scent of their blossom.

It is also in Sleat that traditionalists believed that Gaelic was the universal language in the times before the Tower of Babel.

As the road turns inland and east, passing through birch woods, to rejoin the A85 once more, the Garden of Skye is behind us, with its myths and quiet charm. Perhaps, you may think, the spirit guardians of this area prefer to remain undisturbed, or at least only visited by those who respect and understand its beauty and its history.

Strath and Broadford

Turning left at the junction with the A85 we are, in fact, just a few miles north of Isleornsay and, from here, the main road is wide and fast having recently been improved. To the east is a wild, mainly roadless area; it offers much for the serious walker but is not for the casual stroller. There is, however, a signposted track to the right which leads to a parking area in the **Kinloch Forest**. From here, parked among the ruins of former stone dwellings, lead a number of easier walking routes and there are some stunning views across Loch na Dal. If the visitor is planning a picnic then this offers an excellent stopping place.

Strath, or more properly Strathaird, is MacKinnon country. Sandwiched between the lands of those feuding foes the MacLeods and the MacDonalds, somehow through the centuries the MacKinnons held on to their lands. Skye is wrapped in the stories of endless clan wars between MacLeods and MacDonalds and the MacKinnons must often have felt surrounded but managed to serve, at times, both clans and to marry women from both, retaining their independence and the fertile Strath valley.

Strath landscape holds the ruins of many ancient churches and, often close by, the remains of a number of stone circles, evidence of religious and pagan worship for centuries. The leaflet, *Archaeology of Skye*, available from Tourist Information Centres, plots numerous sites which you can look out for during your travels.

The A85 meets the A87 near Skulamus; to the right lies Skye Bridge, Kyleakin and the road to Kylerhea but that route will be taken later. Instead, turning left onto the A87 we head towards Broadford and the main Strath valley.

Almost immediately after rejoining the A85, to the right, is the little township of Waterloo. Not by chance does this area get its name. When Skyemen returned from the Napoleonic Wars many of them made their home here, by the waters of Broadford Bay, and this area became known as Waterloo; a reminder of the war, and perhaps its greatest land battle, giving its name to the home of returning soldiers.

Broadford, at first sight, appears a sprawling settlement with central services of petrol station, supermarket, veterinary surgeon, bank, restaurants, plus hotels and bed and breakfasts offering accommodation. It is easy to overlook some of the attractions. Skye Serpentarium, for example, signposted left as you enter Broadford offers much to keep children entertained and makes an interesting visit for a wet weather day. It is usually open from Easter to at least late September but do check current opening times; as with many places to visit on Skye, times can vary, dependent on factors such as when Easter falls and the timing of school holidays or mid-term breaks.

In the centre of Broadford is Skye Silver and, just opposite, the lane behind Dunollie Hotel is one of two roads leading to Broadford Bay and its harbour. In fact, the harbourside and bay is an attractive area, has great views and can be a good place for wildlife spotting.

In 2004, staff at Broadford hospital were surprised at two visitors to their Accident and Emergency service. An otter, accompanied by its injured mate, made their way up to the emergency entrance, seeking assistance. The event was captured on camera and featured on the local BBC news programme. The injured otter, with its mate, were cared for by the nearby otter sanctuary before being returned to their natural habitat. Proof that animals may not be as dumb as we may think.

By the harbour the visitor finds a range of craft shops, brightly painted, and well worth exploring. The harbour and bay of Broadford is the jewel of this town.

Walk around Broadford Bay

Park at the main car park on the seafront and, facing the sea, turn left towards the pier. Keep to the path, going through two gates, and you soon start to gain height, reaching Irishman's Point, or Rubh' an Eireannich. From here you can continue along the shore affording views of the little islands and the mainland. There is soon a choice as you reach the next fence. Beyond it lies rather more difficult walking, picking the way along the shore until a forest path is reached which will take you back towards the main road, then left to return to the start. Or you could simply enjoy the views and wander at leisure back by the same route taking in this quiet and scenic area.

West of Broadford, and dominating the town, is Beinn na Callich, part of the **Coire Gorm** horseshoe of three summits. Beinn ne Callich has a large cairn at its peak which is visible for miles around. It can be climbed, as can the entire horseshoe, but is strenuous, ascending over 3,000ft and not to be attempted without adequate equipment and knowledge.

Just by the Broadford hotel, the B8083 is signposted to Elgol and this route is an essential part of any visit to Skye. The road is single track with passing places; it is also a superb route with, at its end, views towards the heart of the dramatic **Cuillin** mountain range; it is arguably one of the best views in an island of imposing and beautiful scenery.

Travelling west through Strath Suardal the road at first follows the Broadford river. After about one mile can be found the ruins of the old house at Coire-chat-achan not far off to the right. This was a MacKinnon country house and in 1773 the MacKinnons entertained Dr Johnson and his companion Boswell during their visit to Skye. Tourist Information Centres stock a leaflet describing Johnson's and Boswell's travels around Skye so that you can follow in their footsteps.

If you park carefully after the first mile there is, to the right, a rough track climbing the small hill of An Sithean. From here is the best view of the ruined house and of Beinn na Callich in the background. At the summit of An Sithean is a stone and there are remnants of a stone circle, once encircling the centre stone.

An Sithean is one of Skye's many 'fairy places'. It is said the fairies dance here on clear moonlit nights and that fairy music can be heard by those with the ears to listen.

Further along this road the visitor passes the ruined church of **Cill Chriosd** and its old graveyard. Nearby is a small stone circle. The graveyard is ancient, and much older than Cill Chriosd church with some slabs still bearing engravings of Celtic design. At one end of the church can still be made out an enclosure

and this, once, was the family burial place of the MacKinnons of Corry.

Loch Cill Chriosd, to the right of the road, completes this pretty spot although the Loch was once haunted by a monster until blessed by St Maelrhuba. Fortunately, since the saint's blessing, the monster is no more and the waters of the Loch calm and pure.

The Deserted Villages

It is from Cill Chriosd that walkers can visit the villages of Boreraig and Suisnish, possibly the most poignant reminders of the highland clearances with their ruined crofts bearing silent testimony to the ruthless cruelty of those events.

The circuit is about 10 miles, and in places the path becomes indistinct and very wet. Although beyond the scope of this book, it is a great days walking and entirely recommended to those who are able and prepared, not only for its history but also for the views, the waterfalls and the opportunity to spot eagles patrolling the crags and slopes of Beinn Bhuidhe.

Continuing our route, the road approaches **Torrin**, where some marble quarrying still takes place, and then on to Loch Slapin.

Less than a mile south east of Torrin and to the north side of Beinn na Dubhaich is high pasture cave. This is a continuing archaeological project at one of Skye's most important prehistoric sites,

Bla Bheinn or Blaven (3,045ft/923m) in The Cuillin from Loch Slapin, near Torrin

dating from late Bronze and Iron Ages.

The site is usually open from April to the end of September and guided tours may be available. The cave, as excavated so far, contains over 320 metres of accessible passages and volunteers each year take part in site fieldwork. Always check with Tourist Information Centres for access and for the special open days which are held in early June and mid September and include demonstrations of prehistoric crafts and skills.

From Torrin there is a magnificent view of **Blaven** (or Bla Bheinn) one of the most photographed mountains and an outlier of the Black Cuillins. Blaven looks as if it could be easy to approach but really is a climb for those who are experienced. An alternative would be to engage the services of Climb Skye mountain guides who know and understand these mountains and who have kindly provided a number of the photographs in this book.

The B8083 continues along Loch Slapin giving a lovely route and climbing above the loch before crossing the Strathaird peninsula.

Walk to An Mam

Near the highest point on this road, at Kilmarie, is a rough track; there is limited parking here and a small plaque announces that the track to **Camusanary** was constructed by M squadron and 107 Field squadron 75 Engineer Regiment (volunteers) in June 1968.

The track is broad and easy to follow, if stony and somewhat uncomfortable to walk. Following this track for almost two miles brings the visitor to one of the most impressive, sublime views available on the Isle of Skye. Although not difficult, this walk is, nevertheless, at the limit of those described in this book. Care must be taken and it is not a route for bad weather. The reward is an outstanding view of sea, mountains and coastline combining to represent the essence of Skye. The walker will pass a cairn marking the top of the Kilmarie to Camasunary pass and soon after, as the track begins its descent, reach the views described above. It is possible to continue downward to Camasunary which entails a much steeper ascent to return by the same route.

The old crofter's cottage, Luib, retaining its thatched roof

As the road nears its end, it descends steeply into **Elgol**, a small settlement which does have a post office, a few shops, refreshments and accommodation.

From Elgol it is possible to walk, and clamber, the coastal route to Camasunary and then on into **Loch Coruisk**. This is a very long route and definitely only for the experienced walker; along the route is the Bad Step, a rock obstacle that requires careful navigation and this route is unsuitable for children.

Most visitors will take advantage of the boat trips from Elgol into Loch Coruisk, ringed by the Cuillin peaks and a contender for 'Britain's Best View'. Taking one of the boat trips is strongly recommended. The two operators, Bella Jane and the Misty Isle boat trips, are adept at spotting the wide range of wildlife that frequent this area. Operating throughout the summer months they run a popular service for climbers taking the boats to begin a traverse of the Cuillin. Various trips of different lengths are available and, in high season, booking is essential. In the author's view this is a trip that simply has to be taken and for most people is the only way to access the heart of the Cuillin.

Close to Elgol and only able to be reached at low tide is Prince Charles' cave. Although the Prince's route and places of hiding around Skye are not always certain, it is generally agreed that this cave is the one in which he hid for six days before leaving Skye for France.

The cave is less than one mile south of Elgol with a path leading from the jetty. Always take great care as the cliff top is fractured in places and can be hazardous. When you reach a rock platform by the shoreline, walk past it, then descend to the shore and return walking along the base of the cliffs. It is a large cave, dark, and almost always full of water

Remember to check the tides as this is definitely a low tide only walk.

Making a leisurely return from Elgol, the visitor arrives again at Broadford. Here, at the junction with the A87, we turn left passing through the traffic lights and heading north once more.

The road continues by the shoreline, firstly of Loch na Cairidh, with the island of Scalpay a short distance offshore. We pass the small settlements of Strollamus, Dunan, and at the point where Loch na Cairidh meets Loch Ainort, ArdDorch. After rounding the headland we reach **Luib** once a picturesque settlement of thatched houses. Sadly, modernisation means that today, slate has replaced thatch as the roofing material of choice.

Skye Blackhouses

Many people believe that a thatched roof means a 'blackhouse'. In fact, the original blackhouses, of which very few remain, are quite different. The traditional blackhouse was identified due to its having a hole in the roof for smoke to escape but no chimney. With peat fires in common use this meant that peat smoke filled the house staining everything black, including the occupants. Peat fires are not the easiest to light and usually would be built up at night to last until morning. The floors of blackhouses were of earth, trampled flat and hens often roosted under the built in bed which filled almost half the room. Blackhouses were a feature of a hard and uncomfortable way of living.

Shortly after Luib there is a choice of two routes both of which, at different times in their history, can lay claim to being the 'new' road. Keeping left on what is now the main A87 this is the rebuilt and much improved route north. Originally a single track road and with a very steep ascent, dangerously sharp turns, and at times becoming more akin to a mountain burn (river) this is Drum na Cleochd. In the early days of motoring it presented a real challenge and, after much hotly contested debate, the decision was taken to build a new road following the course of the loch. This road, now the very minor road signposted Moll, proved dangerous in winter threatening to blow winter users into the loch in bad stormy weather as it clings precariously to the hillside. I have driven a large motorhome along this road in a storm and it proved quite a testing experience.

Ultimately, another new road which, follows in part but not all, of the old Drum na Cleochd road, was built and this incorporates parking areas to let visitors enjoy its wonderful views. It does, still, prove troublesome in snow and ice andmay be closed during snow-storms when it can become impassable for anything but 4x4 vehicles.

As the road descends the visitor reaches **Sconser** and the ferry termi-nal for the short trip to the island of Raasay.

Sconser

Dominated by Glamaig which is the highest and most northerly of the Red Cuillin, Sconser is a natural staging post between south and north Skye and, to the west, the Cuillin and east, the short sea trip to Raasay.

From here there is a route to the summit of Glamaig, just south of the golf course and the junction with the Moll road. It is a route which requires experience demanding a degree of scrambling and coping with the scree slopes. For the experienced it provides, from the summit, a vast and grand panorama taking in Ben Nevis, the Outer Isles, the whole of Raasay and, to the south, Blaven.

Sconser provides accommodation and lunches and dinners are available at the Sconser Lodge hotel with new owners who are keen to raise standards and offer a warm welcome to guests.

West to the Cuillin

Leaving Sconser we drive along the A87 a short distance to **Sligachan**. Look out across Loch Sligachan to the waterfalls tumbling down the steep slopes of Heall Odhar Mor on the opposite shore. Sligachan, and the Sligachan Inn and campsite are a mecca for hillwalkers and, especially, climbers seeking to access the dramatic Cuillin ridges. It is no accident that a mountain rescue post lies just beyond the Sligachan Inn.

Sligachan, with the original Inn built in the 1700s caters for every traveller. There is a large and comfortable hotel, a bunkhouse much loved by climbers, campsite, bar and restaurant. It is a hub of activity for visitors in the summer months.

It is here that the A87, heading for the island capital of Portree, meets the A863 leading west to **Carbost** and then on to Dunvegan.

The old road bridge, Sligachan

Situated at the head of Loch Sligachan and at the head of Glen Sligachan this is the starting point for a number of ascents into the Black Cuillin affording climbs that rival those of the Alps in difficulty if not in actual height.

Glen Sligachan runs from here ending some eight miles away by the sea at Camasunary and divides the gentler Red Cuillin to the east from the dramatic Black Cuillin to the west. Tackling the Black Cuillin is not for inexperienced climbers. There are a number of mountain guiding services such as Climb Skye and, unless you are proficient, experienced and very fit, advice and services from these guides are definitely the best option for anyone determined to make an ascent. Mountain rescue find it necessary to maintain a permanent dog search team on Skye and every year accidents happen; frequently these are due to inexperienced visitors venturing into the Cuillin ridges so please do not add to these sad statistics.

Talisker Distillery

Glen Sligachan

In theory at least, this is a low level and, therefore, relatively simple walk. Signposted from Sligachan and undoubtedly rewarding it is not to be undertaken lightly. For one thing, it is long, very long, almost eight miles and double that distance to return to Sligachan. It is possible, on reaching Camusanary to continue on to Kilmarie or Elgol and to arrange transport from there; however, this increases the level of difficulty at the end of a long route and even through the Glen it can be arduous, hazardous and is usually extremely wet. Often running burns mean taking tiring detours and if undertaken after wet weather the walker may feel they are trudging through eight miles of bog. Nevertheless, it is extremely rewarding, offers views into the corries and therefore the author's best advice would be to ensure you are very well prepared and walk only as far as is comfortable. It is not a route for children. Make sure you have a good walking map and all the equipment previously listed. Keep to the signposted route and remember you will be returning the same distance as already covered.

Just a short way into the Glen, in fine weather, gives a flavour of this area and is always worthwhile but do turn around before tiredness sets in and sooner if the going feels tough.

Broadford from the little quay at Corry on Broadford Bay

From Sligachan, the visitor will notice many signs pointing out the routes to various peaks. Please bear in mind that these are not footpaths and although a short walk along most are a possibility (and a joy) you may soon find yourself out of view of the road and encountering very rough terrain.

At Sligachan we turn left onto the A863 which takes us along Glen Drynoch with the Cuillin away to our left. This is a lovely drive on a good road heading towards the west coast of Skye.

The Ghost Car

Unique in Skye, it is on the road through Glen Drynoch at night that motorists occasionally speak of seeing the headlights of an oncoming car. The headlights are clearly visible but disappear just before reaching the motorist; the oncoming car never materialises. What the origins of the ghost car are no-one knows but it is certainly one of Skye's less than usual ghosts.

As the visitor approaches the west coast the road to the left, the B8009 is signposted to Carbost, Glen Brittle and Talisker Distillery. Turning left here brings you into another area which should not be bypassed.

The B8009 leads to Carbost and Loch Harport; it is also the route to the minor single track road to Glen Brittle and this left turn, less than a mile from the A863 junction, is a popular route towards Glen Brittle beach. Turn here, and take the single track road with care.

It is very popular in summer and passing places must be used carefully and not used for parking. Along this route as it snakes its way gently to the settlement of Glenbrittle are some parking areas. A main one is to the right, rising above the road and about one mile beyond a well signposted sheltered picnic site to the left. The higher parking area is opposite a walking route signed to Sligachan. Parking here gives access to the nine mile circular walking route to Loch Eynort and its return. However, as these are easy walking paths mostly through Forestry Enterprise land it is an excellent place to access a network of pathways worth exploring. From time to time views of the Cuillin appear and wild birds, including eagles, can sometimes be spotted in the vicinity.

From the same car park, cross the road and head for the river. There is a large boulder on the river bank and you should make towards this. As you follow the river's course you encounter the first of a number of waterfalls. The burn flows into a small gorge with cascading falls and many pools.

The Fairy pools are two pools close together divided by a rock arch. Although less than two miles from the car park this is a quiet and beautiful spot, perfect for resting, picnicking, and just enjoying the surroundings. The return is by the same route.

Further along Glen Brittle lies the youth hostel, mountain rescue post and campsite by Glen Brittle beach. Since this is the third of three possible approaches into the Cuillin this is another area in great favour with climbers. The beach itself is one of Skye's largest and a safe place for children to play. There are numerous paths leading from the beach or nearby with walks which make pleasant strolls without being too demanding. Glen Brittle does become busy in the summer but for those visiting outside the high season, as with much of Skye, it is both peaceful and beautiful.

Returning by the single track road, the visitor rejoins the B8009 and turns left into Carbost travelling alongside Loch Harport which glistens pure and vivid under a summer sky.

Carbost is a small village in a perfect location. It has ample accommodation, the popular Old Inn and a small store. It also has a medical centre, the first to be reached on the route since leaving Broadford. Carbost is dominated by Talisker Distillery, which is not in **Talisker**, but is the home of Skye's only malt whisky. Typical of the west coast whiskies, Talisker has that peaty taste which you may love or hate; whiskies from the west of Scotland hold this in common and therefore differ from their east coast counterparts. The distillery is worth visiting and offers tours and tastings and has a small shop. Talisker is open seven days a week in the summer but do remember that Scotland has different laws on alcohol to England and therefore Talisker does not open until mid-day on Sundays.

From Carbost, the first minor road to the left leads to **Loch Eynort**, a gentle drive with the road ending at the small settlement of Eynort lying at the head of the loch. Quiet and largely undisturbed Eynort escapes the attentions of most visitors and, for this reason, retains a solitude which can be difficult to find in summer. From here the forest paths of Glen Brittle are easily accessible and a pleasure to walk.

From just beyond the distillery as the B8009 takes a steep turn to the right the road to Talisker itself is signposted. This picturesque drive ends at Talisker House where a broad path is signposted to Talisker Bay and the beach. The visitor must park carefully here as space is limited and this is also the turning area but from then it is a comfortable walk to the bay and highly recommended. The surrounding cliffs and a waterfall make this a great setting, ideal to sit and spend some time or, perhaps, to watch the sun go down. Birdwatchers often set up cameras and binoculars along the path and are frequently rewarded by visiting seabirds and, occasionally, eagles venturing from the safety of their clifftop homes.

Back at Carbost once more, the B8009 continues to wend its way towards **Portnalong**, two miles further on and then on to Fiskavaig. Portnalong was first settled by weavers from Harris and Lewis in the 1920s and Fiskavaig is a tiny crofting settlement above a stony bay. From here, looking north-west, can just be seen the basalt rock seastacks of MacLeod's Maidens across Loch Bracadale. There is further accommodation here and a youth hostel at Portnalong.

As the visitor travels back along the minor road to rejoin the main A863 there is a sense of leaving the mighty and magnificent Cuillin behind. In fact, as we travel north, unrivalled views of that great range appear in our rearview mirror; stopping to turn and stare is recommended. Meanwhile, we are heading towards the Duirinish peninsula with its soaring cliffs and indented coastline, considered by many to be the jewel in Skye's crown.

2. North Skye

Duirinish & Dunvegan

Continuing the very winding A863 the road shortly hugs the coastline of north-west Skye and ample parking areas are provided along the way. They need to be for every turn along this road brings new and breathtaking vistas; no visitor should venture here without a camera.

As you travel north, stop at intervals and look behind. In addition to the views out to the sea and the islands, the mass of the Cuillin come into view striking a magnificent pose. Soon the visitor is driving alongside **Loch Bracadale** with more islands just offshore and then crossing the bay to reach **Struan**, set above a natural harbour with small craft bobbing in the waters. This small village has accommodation, restaurant and a well-stocked village store. It is also the home of Cioch, an independent outdoor clothing store able to offer sound advice and some of the best clothing suited to the weather and terrain of Skye. From Struan a minor road climbs across the high moors and provides a short cut, indeed the only short cut, to Portree the only town on the island and its capital.

Just beyond Struan is the sign to

North Skye

Rudha Hunish
Duntulm
Skye Museum of Island Life
Flodigarry
A855
Waternish Point
Loch Snizort
Staffin
Kilt Rock
N
W—E
S
Outer Hebrides
Uig
Lealt
Rona
Trumpan
B886
Skyeskyns Exhibition Tannery
A87
Old Man of Storr
Fladday
Stein
The Storr
Piping Museum
Borreraig
A850
Sound of Raasay
Brochel
Loch Pooltiel
Dunvegan Castle
Edinbane
A855
Milovaig
Glendale
B884
Dunvegan
Isle of Raasay
Toy Museum
Neist Point
Colbost Folk Museum
Roag
B885
Aros Experience
Portree
Orbost
Harlosh
Ose
Dun Caan
Struan
Bracadale
A87
Loch Bracadale

0   5 miles
0 5km

Dun Beag with parking to the left of the road. In an island with so many archaeological sites of interest, this is the best preserved broch on Skye as well as being very easily accessible. Although about 2,000 years old the tower and some inner galleries still remain. Its importance as a lookout post is obvious with panoramic views all around.

Just opposite and not far from the car parking area is the relatively well preserved Ullinish souterrain or underground passage. There is still much debate around the original use for these structures; they were well built and clearly of some importance but whether the main purpose was ritual, storage or shelter is still not clear.

Ullinish Point

At this point on the main road is a single track minor road signposted Ullinish. This road takes a loop, away from the main road, towards Ullinish Point before skirting the coast and rejoining the main road at Eabost. The visitor should take this road and drive to the viewpoint by Ullinish Point. From here a grand view across loch and islands towards Ardtreck lighthouse and, in the background, the majestic Cuillin. A great little detour which also takes the visitor by Ullinish Lodge hotel, one of the finest hotels and restaurants on Skye.

Oronsay Island

Take the lane from the road to Ullinish Lodge and, where it ends, go through a gate and onto a rough track which leads to the causeway linking Oronsay island, at low tide, with Ullinish. From this quiet, green island it is possible to watch seals, many seabirds such as gannets, fulmars and gulls, and occasionally a basking shark.

In the distance are MacLeod's Tables, those curious flat-topped hills which overlook Dunvegan and, to the south, Ardtreck, the sea cliffs of Fiskavaig and the Cuillin. Please do remember to check the tide times as Oronsay does become a true island at high tide. The best time to walk across is as the tide is going out giving time to enjoy this peaceful place.

NB. Due to the wildlife presence this walk is not suitable for dogs.

On returning to the main A863 we continue north through the tiny scattered settlement of **Ose** where a number of very good bed and breakfast places offer accommodation for the traveller. This is the head of Loch Caroy and the shore is easily accessible from here; visitors often stroll near the water's edge while local people walk their dogs.

To the right a minor road leads to Balmeanach and on into the forest; Once you reach the edge of the forest the track is suitable only for 4x4 vehicles, so if your suspension is valued, a quiet walk is recommended. At Balmeanach the lovely gardens of Balmeanach House bed and breakfast are, on occasion, open to visitors in the summer months. Check with the Tourist Information Centre for opening times or, alternatively, book accommodation and enjoy the garden as a bonus.

Back on the road as it winds round the head of **Loch Caroy** is a little sign announcing St John's Chapel. Most visitors miss this spot entirely. Here are found the ruins of a tiny Episcopal church, named after St John the Baptist standing silent by the sea within its own graveyard. In winter this graveyard is a carpet of snowdrops.

Legend has it that the graveyard at Caroy was built over a prehistoric burial ground and on fairy ground. It is believed to be haunted and the ghostly presences said to be felt very strongly. Although some say that things can be seen at night none dare tell what those things might be. There are also those who say the fairy songs can be heard rising from the ground.

The next peninsula reached by minor road branching from the A863 is **Harlosh**, another delightful detour. The remains of another broch, Dun Feorlig, lie near to the road and, from lower Harlosh, the Piper's Cave near to Harlosh Point can be reached. There is a youth hostel at Harlosh and more panoramic views along the minor route. The road rejoins at Roskhill where it overlooks Pool Roag. Just before the left turn towards **Roag** is Dun Studio which can be visited almost all year.

Duirinish has two distinct advantages: firstly it can justly claim coastal walking amongst the finest in Britain and secondly, much of its spectacular beauty is relatively accessible. It is no coincidence that the area is home to many artists and craftspeople who take their inspiration from their surroundings and the special qualities of light and shade on Skye.

No trip to Skye would be complete without visiting at least some of the many galleries and studios with which Skye abounds. There truly is something for everyone and, unfailingly, those who work in diverse ways welcome visitors and are keen to share their love of this unique island and how its magic guides their work. The booklet *Elements Of Excellence* is widely available and divided into 'studio trails' making it easy to locate studios and galleries along the visitors' route. Within the pages of this book a number are mentioned; it is not that others are less worthy of attention. Simply there is insufficient space to highlight every studio or craft workshop. Instead, the visitor is urged to discover for themselves the wealth of talent with which Skye abounds.

Turning let at the sign for Roag the visitor takes the minor road leading to this lovely straggling settlement. Follow the road across the head of Pool Roag and uphill where you find Phil Gorton's photographic studio, open all year, and displaying a very personal interpretation of the Skye landscape.

Tea arrives in Roag

It was in Roag that tea first arrived on Skye. A sailor sent a box of tea home to his two aunts who lived in a cottage in Roag. Never having seen tea before they debated long over how it should be served. Eventually deciding that it must be a sort of vegetable they stewed the tea leaves and served them as a vegetable with butter, inviting their neighbours to share in this special Oriental treat. Needless to say all those who shared this meal remained quite unimpressed with the new 'food'.

After the road crosses another burn there is a tiny turning left which leads to Roag's small and stony shore and to Ardroag. Wading birds and otters have been seen here and by Ardroag a corncrake heard. Continuing through Roag newer dwellings mix with the original croft houses until you reach a sharp right hand bend with a lane signposted to Greep. There is a cattle pen here, on the right, and enough room to park carefully. It is worth stopping and taking in the views across Ardroag, Harlosh and Loch Bracadale to the Cuillin beyond. This is a favourite view for artists and you may often find someone at work, seated on the grassy bank. It is a scene which begs to be captured in whichever medium you choose.

The road gains height as it heads towards **Orbost** where the Orbost Gallery sits in a dip and displays work from a number of artists.

At the highest point on this road

some strange events have been reported. Once the site of an old graveyard it is said that here Roag was once haunted by the Gruagach and may still be so. In Skye the Gruagach appeared as a tall thin woman with very long hair and wearing a white misty robe. She was said to be seen when something dire was about to happen and, indeed, at least three unexplained deaths have occurred at this spot as well as ghostly sightings, the last as recent as 2005.

At Orbost the road comes to a T-junction; the road turns right but taking a left turn brings you to the parking area by Orbost House. A sign tells you this is the last public parking at the end of this public road. From here it is an easy walk down to Orbost beach and Loch Bharcasaig. There is a forest at the far edge of the beach part of which is known as Rebel's Wood or the Memorial Woods. This is in memory of Joe Strummer, of The Clash, responsible for the newer planting in collaboration with Future Forests as an example of carbon offsetting. Since Joe's early death a number of visitors arrive each year not only to visit the beach, bay and Rebel's Wood but to pay their respects to an outstanding musician.

MacLeod's Maidens

This is another walk that is at the limits of those described in this book. Although not difficult, it is quite long, about ten miles in total, but the Duirinish coast is so lovely the author would be remiss in not including at least some options on this peninsula.

Walking towards the forest, take the wooden bridge over the burn and follow the broad track through the older forest. Soon you cross the Forse burn and start to ascend; this is the newer Rebel's Wood. There are cairns marking the way and the path continues a gentle climb. It descends again towards Brandarsaig Bay and from there takes you to the deserted crofts of Brandarsaig. The path is quite clear, leading on to the ruins of Idrigill and then towards Idrigill Point. From here head to the cliff top for the best view of MacLeod's Maidens and beyond.

According to legend the three maidens are the wife and two daughters of the fourth Chief of Clan MacLeod who died here when their boat was smashed on the rocks and sunk.

It is possible from here to continue on and, indeed, to walk the whole of the Duirinish coast but that is a major undertaking not to be attempted without experience and meticulous planning for the twenty six mile journey.

Orbost House and farm are also a possible starting point for those wishing to ascend MacLeod's Tables with another route starting further along the Orbost to Dunvegan road. These can be a strenuous ascent requiring a degree of skill and experience.

From Orbost car park return to the junction and continue straight ahead. The road meanders along for a couple of miles, passing an alternative route to MacLeod's Tables until, to the left, is signposted the B884 leading to Glendale.

Glendale is a village but also the term for the region furthest north-west on the Duirinish peninsula. Very popular with those settling here from other parts of Britain, Glendale is sometimes referred to as Little England.

Musicians and Festivals

Joe Strummer is not the only well known musician with links to Skye and the island is not short on home-grown talent either.

For almost twenty years the Strathaird peninsula was owned by Iain Anderson, flautist and front-man of Jethro Tull. More recently K T Tunstall recorded an album on Skye and she has played at the Skye Music Festival.

During the 1960s Donovan founded a community on the Waternish peninsula which, although short lived, attracted a number of musicians to the island.

In modern times Runrig are probably the best known Celtic group and Skye is also home to the Peat Bog Faeries who have a strong following; it is often possible to catch one of their local gigs during a visit to Skye.

The island has a strong tradition of piping which dates back to the sixteenth century. Skye, and Duirinish, were home to the MacCrimmons, hereditary pipers to the Clan MacLeod. Some of their pibrochs (long Gaelic laments) are hailed as the greats of Scottish and Gaelic culture. In early August each year pipers compete for the Dunvegan Silver Chanter at Dunvegan Castle, ancestral home of Clan MacLeod.

Annually, the Skye Music Festival held at Ashaig airstrip (no airport) near Broadford, attracts an influx of visitors, making accommodation in late May very difficult to find. Other local festivals celebrate traditional music including the Pipe Band Festival (late June), Edinbane Festival (early July), Skye Festival (various events mid to late July) and the Accordion and Fiddle Festival (late May) in Portree. As times and dates become confirmed the local What's On guide informs you of these events. Near Portree, the Aros Centre holds various concerts throughout the year and a number of hotels and inns regularly host live music. Ceilidhs can be held anywhere from an hotel to a village hall; ask at the local Tourist Information Centres or look in the local newspaper, the West Highland Free Press, for details.

Just a short way along the B884 a minor road signposted to Uiginish leads to the right. For a perfect view of Dunvegan castle across Loch Dunvegan a drive along this road is worthwhile.

Further on, another minor road takes the visitor to **Borreraig** and then close to Dunvegan Head. At Borreraig, by the memorial cairn to the MacCrimmons, is Borreraig Park where you can discover the history of the pipers as well as life in bygone days. Also here is the studio of Diana Mackie who creates unique designs in jewellery. At the end of this road lies Galtrigill and the remains of another deserted village.

Galtrigill, then called Galtrigal, was the home of Donald MacLeod. After Culloden it was he who managed to transport Bonnie Prince Charlie safely to Uist and was responsible for his safekeeping until handing him on to Flora MacDonald. Donald MacLeod went even further in serving his Prince; keenly aware of the hunt for the Prince he distracted attention by going off alone and drawing the hunt away from Prince Charlie's true route. Donald was, almost inevitably such was the fervent search for the Prince, captured on Benbecula and confined to a prisonship for many long months. Eventually released in 1747 he returned to his Galtrigill home a dying man.

A mile along the track from Galtrigill is the Manners Stone. Traditionally anyone who walks three times to the stone and then rests on it will find their manners.

Returning to the B884 the visitor arrives at **Colbost** with its Croft Museum, Raven Press gallery and the world famous Three Chimneys restaurant. The Three Chimneys is open for lunch and dinner and, in peak season, it is essential to book in advance. A mile further on is the old schoolhouse which is now Skye Silver; a popular choice for tourists seeking something different in silver jewellery.

The road drops sharply into the scattered village of Glendale with another minor road, left, following the course of Glen Dale and the Hamara river which runs through the valley. Glendale has a village stores, post office and café as well as a range of accommodation. There is also the Toy Museum which houses an eclectic mix of toys from many decades. All amenities are central and parking is provided in a village car park.

From Glendale the B road continues to Lower Milovaig and Meanish, with tiny Meanish Pier on Loch Pooltiel itself bordered by high cliffs and waterfalls. There is a gentle ambience here, as well as a number of easy walks in and around the village and the coast. It does make Glendale, as with Roag, one of those delightful places for evening strolls. If you are lucky you may spot an otter in Loch Pooltiel or a bird of prey hunting for food. Both golden eagles and white tailed sea eagles nest among the high sea cliffs of this area.

Most visitors come this way en route to visiting Neist Point which is an undoubtedly a spectacular spot with stunning views and, often, excellent chances of spotting dolphin, minke whales or even basking shark in the waters off the point. Its beauty and its fame mean that at times in the summer it can become very overcrowded. A suggestion would be to visit late afternoon or early evening; even later, watching the sun go down from here is highly recommended.

There is, nowadays, a small car park at Neist Point and from here an easy concrete path leads out to the lighthouse. It is then possible to cross the grass plateau and down to the edge of the sea but do take care. Expect to be windswept around Neist Point as it bears the brunt of some of Skye's fiercest winds.

This most westerly part of Skye is a wonderland for bird watchers. There are many walks to Waterstein Head and to Ramasaig cliffs, as well as from Neist Point itself. On all of these, binoculars and camera are part of the essential equipment to watch the diversity of birdlife living or visiting these soaring cliffs.

Winding back towards **Dunvegan** gives tantalizing glimpses of the castle from across Loch Dunvegan long before reaching the main A863. Dunvegan is a small village which is host to large numbers of visitors each year. As a result it has post office, bakery/café, an excellent village store, another store specializing in organic and vegetarian produce, news agency and store and, since 2008, a local cobbler. In addition the Highland Ordnance shop is an Aladdin's cave with a range of fishing equipment, camping essentials, outdoor clothing and a host of other supplies.

Dunvegan has accommodation for every traveller from hotels to bunkhouse and one of the two Tourist Information Centres on Skye which are open all year (the other is in Portree). Along the route given in this book this is also the place with the first available petrol since leaving Broadford.

Just across the road from Tourist Information is the church of Scotland and the start of the popular 'Two Churches Walk'. An information leaflet is available from the Information Centre. This is an easy and rewarding walk of less than one hour, which is accessible for most people and suitable for children. It takes in woodland paths as well as higher open ground with lovely views and passes close to the Duirinish Stone and the old ruined church of St Mary's. It is also popular with local people walking their dogs.

Skye at Night

The far northwest of Skye is one of those rare places in Britain, which has no light pollution meaning that many more stars can be seen in the night sky; even the Milky Way can be visible with the naked eye. Occasionally the Northern Lights, or Aurora Borealis, make an appearance; the best times for this phenomenon are spring and autumn when columns of moving lights can appear over Dunvegan Head.

In summer the days are long and the stars fade between the end of April and mid-August, a time when the sun never drops more than 18 degrees below the horizon. In mid-summer it is possible to see outside all night; this is the period between 23rd May and 21st July when nautical twilight is never reached. Nautical twilight is the point when the sun dips 12 degrees and more below the horizon. When this does not happen true darkness never falls.

The ruined St Mary's Church and John McLeod's monument of 1745 near to the Duirinish Stone

Duirinish Stone

This great stone, high on the hill overlooking Dunvegan is not, as may be thought, of prehistoric origin. The stone is fifteen foot high and weighs five tons and, it was erected to mark the millennium. Using the same techniques as were used thousands of years ago to erect stone circles, incredibly the villagers of Dunvegan used just ropes and manpower to drag the stone into place and erect it on midsummer's day of the year 2000. It was an impressive feat.

A visit to Dunvegan Castle is recommended. From the large car park the entrance is across the road where the visitor finds the gardens, grounds and castle itself. The gardens are particularly splendid and as they continue to the edge of the loch, look out for seals, which may be spotted. The ancestral home of Clan MacLeod, the castle has been on this spot, in one form or another, since AD1200. As it appears today the castle dates from the 14th, 16th and 17th centuries; it also underwent some remodelling in the 1840s. It is said to be the oldest residence in Britain continuously occupied by generations of the same family and there are a number of rooms open to visitors.

Almost alone amongst landowners in the highlands, the MacLeods did not, during the times of the clearances, sweep their clans people from their hereditary lands to make way for the more profitable sheep.

The Fairy Flag is the most treasured

possession of Clan MacLeod. Long ago, after a clan chief married a fairy thinking she was mortal they lived happily together for twenty years. At the end of twenty years her allotted time with mortals came to an end and she had no choice but to return to her own people. In compensation for his loss the fairies presented him with the silk Fairy Flag. It is said to have the power to save the clan from destruction but only on three occasions. So far it has been used, and has worked, twice; at the battle of Glendale in 1490 and at Trumpan in 1578. From later tests, it seems the flag was actually made around AD600 in the Middle East.

Follow the road past Dunvegan Castle, from which point it quickly becomes a single track and it winds its way towards the small crofting settlement of Claigan.

Along the way, immediately after the road crosses a causeway, is a small parking space. If you stop here and carefully follows the track on the left, which passes between two small mounds, it leads to the waters edge by two of the many islets of Loch Dunvegan. This is an excellent place to watch for the seals which frequent the rocks and islets of

Two views of Dunvegan Castle

the loch. An alternative is to take one of the seal boat trips which leave from a point, from the village, just before the castle entrance.

At the end of this minor road a car park is provided and from here a well defined path leads to the coral beaches, a unique feature of Skye, and immensely popular. These beaches glisten, reflect light and look just like coral. In fact they are composed of tiny particles of a form of seaweed. However, on a bright summer day it is easy to forget their true origin and believe this is a true coral beach such as may be found in the West Indies.

Returning to Dunvegan the A850 takes the visitor away from the north-west coast and starts its journey east towards Portree.

Three miles further the B886, to the left, is signposted to Waternish penin-sula. By this turning is another of Skye's fairy places: **Fairy Bridge**. This is said to be the place where the fairy wife of another clan chief took her leave of her mortal husband to return forever to the fairies. The presence of the fairies here makes this place unsettling for horses. Many accounts tell of horses shying away from the bridge as they can see and hear the fairies dancing. Visitors are advised to wish the fairies well as they pass for fear of upsetting them and bringing bad luck if they fail to acknowledge the fairies kindly.

Waternish

Waternish is a wild and beautiful place offering undisturbed solitude to those who walk its hills. Two miles from Fairy Bridge the first sight of Loch Bay comes

Walking in Waternish

This is frequently a matter of finding your own way. There are almost no clear paths so the few walkers who trouble to explore the inland hills and Waternish Point must, by and large, fashion their own route. Of those that do exist to some degree the way to Waternish Point is, with the help of sheep tracks, a walk of interest as well as the remarkable views which abound.

From the car park at **Trumpan** church, follow the road north until the sharp bend. At this point go through a gate on the left onto a broad track. After passing another gate there is a large cairn, which commemorates John MacLeod killed in a battle on Waternish, in about 1530. Just a short way further on is the memorial cairn to his son, Roderick, who died in the same battle.

After walking further Dun Borrafiach may be seen. This is one of the better preserved brochs of Skye and, nearby but in a state of ruin, is Dun Gearymore. From here, what track there is approaches the ruined croft houses of Unish and it is easy to find the way to the lighthouse at the Point from here. Standing at the Point you can look across to the seacliffs of Duirinish, the Outer Isles are visible and you may be rewarded by sighting marine mammals or those birds who live undisturbed in this little visited corner of Skye.

into view with, often, numbers of small craft in its waters. Shortly, the visitor reaches **Stein** (pronounced steeen), a picture perfect village, now a conservation area, set by a stony beach on Loch Bay. Originally built as a fishing village, in an attempt to organize the fishing industry, today Stein is a free crofting township.

There is accommodation on offer, excellent seafood dining at the Loch Bay restaurant and Dive and Sea Hebrides offer a range of diving excursions and experiences. Stein has a gallery and, overlooking the bay, the Stein Inn, Skye's oldest inn and a great favourite with locals and visitors alike. If you arrive early then a window table may be available to enjoy the views; in good weather there are also tables outside on the grassy bank just above the beach.

Set just above the village and by the road is Skyeskins, a traditional exhibition tannery where the workshop is open to visitors. Further on is Shilasdair with its range of designer sweaters and some of the loveliest yarns available; both are well worth visiting.

The road effectively ends, turning back on itself, at Trumpan church. There is a car park here and glorious windswept views. Trumpan is in a fairly ruined state and has been for some time, but its position is unsurpassed. From here it is a short walk, about one mile, to Ardmore Point from where it is often possible to watch seals at play in the waters below.

In May 1578, MacDonalds from Uist quietly sailed into Ardmore Bay. It was a Sunday and the MacLeods were at prayer in Trumpan church. The MacDonalds crept up to the church, barricaded the door, and set fire to the thatched roof. The fire spread quickly through the church killing everyone inside with the exception of one girl who escaped. This act was a direct reprisal for a massacre, by the MacLeods, of 395 MacDonalds on the Isle of Eigg in 1577.

The young girl who escaped ran back to Dunvegan and raised the alarm. MacLeods from Dunvegan raced to attack the galleys of the MacDonalds which were still at Ardmore Bay, stranded by the low tide. The MacLeods had brought with them the Fairy Flag which they held high as they attacked the raiding MacDonalds.

There were too many dead MacDonalds to bury so the nearby stone wall (or dyke) was simply pushed over to cover the mound of bodies. For this reason the battle is usually referred to as 'the Battle of the Spoiled Dyke'. Of course the MacLeods success in defeating their enemy gave further weight to the magical qualities of their Fairy Flag.

Returning from this quiet corner, steeped in history, the visitor arrives back at the main A850 and turns left towards **Edinbane**. About a mile and a half along this road, on the left, is a parking area marked Greshornish. The gate here leads to a long path in part forested and in part with superb views across to Uig Bay. The entire route is a seven mile circular walk taking in Greshornish Point and is one of the driest paths on Skye; as well as being suitable for the most part for cycling, it is also a great favourite with local people walking their dogs.

Opposite Greshornish is the site of Skye's first wind farm just by Edinbane. Eventually given planning approval

Above: View towards Waternish Point

Below: Monastic cell remains, St Columbas Isle
Inset: Old grave, St Columbas Isle

Two views of Loch Greshornish

after much debate and in the face of strong opposition from Edinbane residents it is, thankfully, a small development although visible from much of northern Skye. Ironically, the one place from which the wind turbines cannot be seen is Edinbane.

Edinbane is a small community, now bypassed by the main road with a shop and accommodation. It is home to Edinbane pottery with its wood kilns and attractive craft shop and to the Edinbane Lodge, a lovely old inn set by the bridge over the Abhainn Choisleader river which flows into Loch Greshornish. As at Dunvegan, the camping and caravan site at Edinbane is perfectly situated at the edge of the loch; both are well placed for exploring north Skye.

The A850 continues its route east passing small townships along the way. For another idyllic view and photo opportunity, take the minor road to Kildonan which, as it almost reaches the cliff edge gives the best views across Loch Greshornish towards Greshornish Point to the west and the headland dividing it from Loch Snizort to the east. The minor road makes a loop back to rejoin the main road quite quickly. As it proceeds it passes little Loch Treaslane and the loch side township of Bernisdale. If the visitor is following an Ordnance Survey map then 'sheepdog trials' is marked at Bernisdale. Unfortunately this is now out of date. A local man, once a successful participant in the BBC programme One Man and his Dog used to give demonstrations but has retired in recent years.

After passing Snizort and crossing the Snizort river there is a minor road on the left signposted Tote and Prabost. Although nothing else is signposted if you turn left here and immediately sharp left again into a lane this will take you to **St Columba's Isle**. Park carefully along the lane and walk towards the building; as you approach the gates, turn right and soon the old bridge, a small island with ruined remains of an old chapel and a new bridge are in sight. The Snizort river tumbles along below you and makes this a very pleasant walk. Crossing the bridge to the island reveals a number of very old graves including one, apparently, of a mediaeval knight amidst others of great antiquity.

The ruined chapel is dedicated to St Columba who visited Skye around AD585 and this tiny island is a gem to explore. Most visitors remain unaware of its existence and, being unmarked from the main road, its silent emptiness serves to add to the sense of history and calm that prevails.

The A850, at Borve, joins the A87, north to Uig and the Trotternish peninsula and south to the island capital of Portree.

Trotternish

At first the main road into Trotternish pushes gently north giving little clue to the stark, strange and unique features of this peninsula of Skye. The area holds a number of standing stones and other relics of its prehistoric past. Central to the peninsula is the great Trotternish ridge, which is a popular long distance path. Its length means that an overnight stay under the stars is required to complete the traverse from north to south.

To the left a minor road leads to Tote which has a Pictish symbol stone not far from the road. Another with a similar symbol carving can be found at Dunvegan castle.

The first settlement along the A87 in this direction is Kensaleyre. Here is found Cairn Liath; a large burial cairn with chambers within which human bones were found. A short distance further, at Eyre, are the Eyre standing stones. These stones are thought to date from the Bronze Age and legend tells that they were once used to support the huge cooking pot of the mythical giants, the Fiene, and used to cook their venison stews.

The road crosses the Romesdal and Hinnisdale rivers both of which are known for the good trout fishing which they provide. Kingsburgh settlement is notable in that the stretch of road from here to Uig is the oldest road on Skye. It is noted in a government survey of 1799 as being 'a good horse road'.

Nearby, after crossing the Hinnisdale river is Caisteal Uisdean, otherwise known as Hugh's castle. Built by Hugh MacDonald of Sleat during the reign of James VI this is said to be the last mediaeval castle to be built on Skye. It occupies a fine location by the shoreline and was, once, an imposing building.

Hugh MacDonald was well known as a rogue and someone not to be trusted. When the castle was completed he saw an opportunity to plot against a foe by inviting him, and others, to a gathering at his new abode. He ordered letters to be sent to his intended victim inviting him to the castle and another letter to a hired murderer giving instructions to rid MacDonald of his foe. Things did not turn out as MacDonald planned because the two letters were mixed up each going to the wrong recipient and giving ample warning to the proposed victim. The result was that Hugh himself was seized and imprisoned in Duntulm castle at the northern tip of Trotternish. He was reportedly fed only salt meal and fish and given no water at all until he died in agony.

As the route approaches **Uig** there are wonderful views across the bay and from an obvious vantage point close to the Uig hotel and high above the village visitors can watch the Calmac ferries as they travel between Uig and the Outer Isles of Harris and North Uist. Many visitors take the opportunity to extend their trip and spend at least a couple of days visiting the islands. The service from Uig pier began with passenger steamer services in 1840 and the car ferry was operational by 1963.

Uig itself has accommodation, including a small campsite, village shop, café and a petrol station. By the pier are Uig pottery and Skye Brewery. Both are a worthwhile visit and, in particular, Skye Brewery as its real ales of Black Cuillin and Red Cuillin are excellent real ales.

Uig and the area around offers a number of walks and these are fairly easy, short walks suitable for most visitors. From Uig village the A87 ends and as the road which continues it way north starts to climb from here it is the A855 and at times comes close to qualifying as single track.

Duntulm Castle Hotel, with the Outer Hebrides on the horizon

Sròn Vourlinn near Dunans, north of Staffin

Short walks by Uig

1. From the hairpin bend at the start of the A855 you will see a gate. Taking the path through this leads out to Idrigill and is a scenic and gentle walk.

2. On the A855 there is a stile next to the bridge over the river Rha quite close to the beginning of the road. This leads to a short walk which is steep but has steps to a beautiful waterfall.

3. A short coastal wander is found by taking the rising gate just by the village store on the A87 as you enter Uig. The path takes you through the woods and then along the shoreline. A return can be made by the same route, directly along the main road or by crossing the footbridge and walking along the playing field.

4. At the Uig hotel just before entering Uig there is a turning almost immediately before the hotel, park along here and walk the remainder of the route to Balnaknock and Fairy Glen. Here the landscape is of numbers of small mounds and quite different to the land the visitor has become accustomed to journeying around north Skye. It is a landscape in miniature and a great place for children to play. The small hillocks are known as fairy hills giving the area the name of Fairy Glen.

From Uig, keeping to the A855, the road turns inland for a time with some fine views out to sea along the way. By Totescore a small headland juts out to sea and this is the point where Bonnie Prince Charlie, dressed as a serving maid to Flora MacDonald, landed and waited for Flora to meet him and take him to the safety of Kingsburgh House where he stayed for a short time. Just after Linicro, if the visitor has been reading a map, it will be noticed that Loch Chaluim Chille is marked but nowhere to be seen. It is the site of a loch which was drained in 1825 to provide rich arable land. The loch used to have its own island and it is believed that St Columba founded a chapel here. Later a monastery was founded at the same spot.

One mile further is Kilvaxter and the site of a recently discovered souterrain (underground passage) which is still being excavated and can be visited just close to the road.

The next settlement is **Kilmuir** and home of the Museum of Island Life. Arranged as seven thatched cottages, this unique museum is great fun as well as informative and open from Easter to October. To the rear is a cemetery and the imposing memorial stone cross to Flora MacDonald above her grave.

Kilmuir is name which indicates the presence, at some time, of a church and the same applies to Kilmuir (now Kilmuir road) by Dunvegan and to Kilmore in Sleat. The church here was dedicated to St Moluac and the river here, Kilmoluag, recalls his name. In Gaelic Kilmuir translates as the land of cream.

The road now drops quickly and steeply towards the coastline before climbing again towards **Duntulm**.

Just a little way offshore lies the island of Fladda Chuan which is believed to be the location of the island of Perpetual Youth. St Columba is thought to have built a chapel here with a great altar stone made of black rock. Originally a Druid stone it was also known as the weeping stone due to being constantly wet. Following superstition, until fairly recent times, fishermen would land on the island and pour three handfuls of sea water over the stone. This was believed to prevent flooding and to bring favourable winds.

As the road climbs and reaches the northern headland of Trotternish there is a large parking area by the ruins of Duntulm castle. This was originally the site of a Pictish fort and the castle over many years frequently changed hands between the MacLeods and the MacDonalds depending on which clan was in the ascendancy at the time. The castle finally rested with the MacDonalds in 1539 and was an impressive sight with 50ft cliffs on three sides and a sea gate as its second entrance. This was an impregnable fortress. It was eventually deserted about 1730 and the MacDonalds quarried much of its stone to build a new home at Monkstadt. At the entrance to the castle, a short walk from the parking area, is a memorial to the MacArthurs, hereditary pipers to clan MacDonald.

Rubha Hunish is the most northerly point of Skye and one of the best places to watch passing dolphins, whales and other visitors as well as an array of birdlife. It is however, difficult to reach involving a descent down the craggy face of Meall Tuath. Such a splendid viewpoint is worth the effort for those who are fit and well prepared. If that is too much to contemplate, then walking from the path around the castle will take you north along the shore of Tulm Bay and the top of Meall Tuath is easy to find from there. Scanning and enjoying the spectacular panorama from here is almost as good and a safer option. This walk does take you close to the cliff edges so please remember to take care; in adverse weather visiting the castle is sufficient.

The road now crosses the headland taking an inland route and passes Shulista, home of the MacLeans who were hereditary doctors to the MacDonalds.

Shulista was also the site of Skye's first school founded in 1610. As well as teaching maths and navigation the school apparently majored in languages, teaching its pupils English, Gaelic, Greek and Latin.

Soon after the sharp bend, the one with the red telephone box on the corner, a minor road leads down to Port Gobhlaig, a pretty little spot by the sea at Kilmaluag Bay and always very quiet. There is parking and this sheltered place is a good choice for picnics and just resting awhile.

The A855 turns to the south and heads down the Trotternish coast. A number of islands enhance the sea views and the road reaches **Flodigarry**. The Flodigarry hotel here was once home to Flora MacDonald long before its present incarnation as a popular hotel. Flodigarry is also one starting point for those energetic walkers wishing to traverse the length of the Trotternish ridge or walking up into the **Quiraing**,

that wonderland of strange rock shapes that beg to be explored.

Less than a mile south of Flodigarry by the parking space is the Loch Siant Well. Believed to be the most famous spring on Skye it is said to be a wishing well and folk would leave offerings of small items such as rags, coloured threads and pins to bring good luck.

As the road heads toward **Staffin** views of the wild and contorted rock formations of the Quiraing become clearer. Immediately before Staffin is Digg where, along the shore, the fossil of an ichthyosaurus was discovered in 1966. It was taken for display to the Royal Museum of Scotland in Edinburgh. Staffin is a settlement of fair size and spread over a wide area. It has Staffin Bay, possibly the most beautiful bay on Skye and the place where dinosaur prints where discovered. These are now on show at Staffin's small but very interesting museum. Not for nothing is this known as the Jurassic coast of Skye.

From Staffin a closer visit to the Quiraing is made possible by taking the minor road to the right as you reach about the centre of this township. This minor road climbs rapidly in a series of bends. After quite a sharp hairpin as the road straightens there is parking to the left. Driving this road gives great views from the rear view mirror which is one reason why the author recommends taking a return by the same route.

Whatever walking ability the visitor has from this car park, even a short walk into the Quiraing will reveal some strange formations. These were formed by pressure on the sedimentary rocks by the lava layers, resulting in massive

View from Quiraing down the Trotternish Ridge

Staffin Museum

Mealt Falls and Kilt Rock in the distance

landslips and in the odd shapes we see today.

Cross the road from the car park where a clear and well used path is obvious and where the first rocks are reached in just over half a mile. On the right is the Prison, a rocky wedge with cliffs on one side and a steep grassy bank on the other. Near the Prison is the Needle standing 120ft high. The Table is not far from here but exploration requires some scrambling and straying far from the path is not for the inexperienced. Taking the path this far gives an impression that will remain but for walkers it is at this point that retracing your steps is recommended. Nor is any part of this walk to be attempted in bad weather or poor visibility since there are sharp drops between crags and the Quiraing can be a dangerous place.

One of the formations among those of the Quiraing is known as the Cup. In days gone by it was well known as a safe hiding place for cattle in troubled times when cattle might be stolen or 'rustled' as it was sufficiently large to hold a herd of reasonable size. The reason for this is the narrow entrance which if necessary could be held against attack by just two or three men. Happily it no longer needs to be used for this purpose.

The drive from Staffin towards Portree is full of opportunities to explore and numerous parking places are provided along the route for visitors to stop and take advantage of the natural beauty all around.

Following the road south, **Kilt Rock** is signposted from the main road. It is formed from black basalt columns which create folds and, to some, appear much as would the folds of a traditional kilt. Coupled with its horizontal strata or bands this gives the appearance of a tartan pattern and another reason for its name.

The best view of Kilt Rock is from nearby **Mealt Falls** which is nearby. Again there is parking here and the waterfall crashes down the high cliffs with tremendous force. On very windy days the force of wind power is so strong that the water can be seen being blown back up the face of the cliff!

'Fire Hill'

By the road here is Loch Mealt which is surrounded by a number of duns or brochs forming what has been described as a protective ring around the loch. One of these, Dun Beag, is believed to have been a 'Fire Hill' once, one of many across Skye and the highlands whose beacons would be lit to call the men of the clans to arms. It is generally accepted that these 'Fire Hills' were last used in the Jacobite uprising of 1745.

Further on, past the little settlement of Ellishader, lies **Lealt Falls** and, on the coast, Inver Tote. Inver Tote itself is a peaceful little bay which, although only a few hundred yards from the main road feels quiet and remote. It is here that the Lealt river makes its way to the sea and on a summers day is a pleasant place, much more pleasant than the roadside parking area, to rest awhile.

From the parking area at Lealt it is fairly easy to follow the route of the old Diatomite railway, now disused, and there is an information board giving the history of the Diatomite which was carried by the narrow 2ft guage railway from Loch Cuithir to a factory at Inver Tote. The line was constructed in 1887 and closed in 1915 after men left the area at the start of the first World War. The path on this walk is clear and not difficult and leads to a bridge just past Loch Cuithir, nestling beneath crags and cliffs which are normally only seen by climbers; a route well worth taking for the surprisingly good views by the loch.

As the visitor travels along this road it is impossible not to notice the outline of the **Old Man of Storr** as it comes into view, appearing larger at each turn of the road. The **Storr** is the highest point of the Trotternish ridge and it is the Sanctuary, below its cliffs, where the array of pinnacles which includes the Old Man of Storr is found. There is car parking by the forest which borders the A855 and some paths to walk in the forest itself. Most visitors will take their photographs of the Old Man from a distance when he appears to stand sentinel over the lochs of the Trotternish coast.

Always check the information boards for information on the forest paths. Most suffered years of neglect and although a number have been reopened it is worth checking for current information. One route, which is little over one mile, to the Sanctuary, starts to the south of the forest, over a stile where you can reach the top edge of the forest and then on to the Sanctuary. The Old Man is 165ft in height and was not climbed until 1955. This is hardly surprising since it rises as a vertical pillar with an overhang to make

ascent more difficult. There are other pinnacles including the Needle. The Sanctuary is basically an amphitheatre backed by the dark cliffs of the Storr. It is a fascinating place and, ambitions of climbing the Old Man aside, easy to reach and to explore.

Near here is Holm Island, which is described in the Introduction of this book. Almost opposite, although you may wish to move the car and make room for other visitors, there is a bus stop and a sign for the Storr Lochs Power Station. Turn in here and park by the dam. Walking over the dam reveals a path to the viewpoint and beach path and across the bay can be seen the cliffs and waterfalls. This is Bearraig Bay. There is good view of the Old Man from here. The path to the beach is quite steep, so it can be slippery in wet weather but with care takes you to a stony beach which has good fossil hunting possibilities. There is also a grassy area for resting or picnicking.

In 1891 a discovery of treasure was made at **Bearraraig Bay**. The treasure included bracelets, brooches, neck rings and ingots together with a large quantity of Anglo Saxon pennies which dated from the AD900. In all there were 28 objects, over 90 pennies and 18 silver coins. It seems likely that the hoard was hidden away by a Norse seafarer who never returned to collect his loot.

The main road now crosses Loch Leathan on its way to Portree, just seven miles south, the capital of the island and, inevitably the one place almost every visitor reaches at some point in their travels.

The Old Man of Storr

View of the Old Man of Storr over Loch Leathan

The Sound of Raasay, Portree

Portree Harbour

Portree

One important date in the history of Portree is 1540, when King James V visited bringing with him a fleet of warships to anchor in Portree's harbour; he hoped to persuade the clans of Skye to support him. Clan chiefs came to the town to swear an oath of loyalty which, to a large degree, they kept although keeping peace with one another was never seen as part of the bargain.

The name Portree, in Gaelic Port an Righ, means the King's Port and its name dates from that time; previously it was known as Kiltraglen.

Portree is an attractive town and it's harbour with the many coloured buildings on the seafront is especially so. Surrounded by cliffs and high ground the harbour is still much used by fishing boats and pleasure craft. Portree main town lies above the harbour and is centred around Somerled Square where most buses stop and there is car parking near to the war memorial. Just off Somerled Square is the leisure centre with its swimming pool and somewhere to take the children on a rainy day. Leading in the opposite direction is Wentworth Street named after Sir Geoffrey Wentworth, third Lord MacDonald who made his mark in history by eloping to Ireland with the illegitimate daughter of a royal duke. Today, Wentworth Street has many shops which serve visitors seeking refreshment or souvenirs. Most stock locally made crafts and goods and are worth exploring.

Portree does, of course, have a full range of accommodation and the Tourist Information Centre, the largest on the island, is open all year. The towns other main street, Bank Street, runs parallel and above the harbour and here is found the Royal Hotel. Formerly known as MacNabs Inn, this is the place where Bonnie Prince Charlie finally said farewell to Flora MacDonald in 1746. A window in the local Episcopal church has a memorial window dedicated to Flora.

During the 1700s many people left from Portree for North America, leaving behind a life of poverty. Skye at that time had a much greater population than today, almost five times as many lived on the island and departures from the harbour became commonplace. In 1771, to help the people, Sir James MacDonald developed Portree as a fishing port and probably prevented greater emigration by his action.

There are several excellent restaurants in Portree and at the pier the visitor can purchase fresh seafood locally caught. Unsurprisingly seafood is a feature of many restaurants and you are often eating fish caught that morning and cooked by evening.

To the south of the harbour is a peninsula known as The Lump; once upon a time is was the place where public hangings took place, now it provides a central green space, the site of the Highland Games and a short pleasant walk around the headland. Skye Highland Games are held at Portree in August each year and have been since 1877. Today they are opened by the Isle of Skye Pipe Band marching from Somerled Square; anyone visiting Skye at the time of the games should try to see this annual event.

From the centre of Skye a short circular walk of just over two miles starts from the car park just beyond the sign for the Cuillin Hotel. Take the tarmac path signposted to the jetty and beyond the jetty cross the wooden bridge and go through the gate onto the gravel path. This route follows the point with good views back towards the harbour and across the sound to the island of Raasay. When the path starts a zigzag ascent and turns left follow it to rejoin the dyke and keep left, passing farmhouses and with Portree now in sight. The path drops into woodland and soon you are back amongst the houses of the town going downhill and back to the start.

Close to Portree is the Aros Centre which houses shops, restaurant, exhibitions, art gallery, information centre and much to spend a day, especially if the weather is poor and children need to be kept amused. There is also a play area. Various concerts and other events are hosted throughout the year and checking the What's On guide or enquiring at Tourist Information is recommended.

By the car park at Aros Centre is a small forested area with way marked walks and information about the different types of trees and their Gaelic names. These are easy short walks and great for children to explore the woods. They are also popular with local people walking their dogs.

After leaving **Aros Centre** there is a left turn to the Braes. Take this road to the car parking at the Braes itself. Half

a mile or so before the road ends gives the option of walking along this coastal minor road to Loch Sligachan and then on along the shores of the loch. The Braes are an isolated community and this walk along Loch Sligachan is often overlooked but well recommended.

During the crofters' struggle for their lands and their survival in the 1800s a bloody battle took place at the **Braes**. In 1882 a strong force of police constables drafted in from Glasgow arrived with the intention of arresting the crofters for the crime of grazing their cattle on land which had been theirs for generations. As many of the menfolk were at sea the women of the community joined in the fierce fighting that ensued and were said to have 'fought like Amazons'. Eventually the police succeeded in arresting the crofters and taking them away to Portree. The battle caused a great deal of publicity and soon after, in 1883 the Royal Commission was set up. This resulted in uncovering the dreadful conditions crofters suffered and the *Crofters' Holding Act* of 1886 giving rights to tenure and fair rent to the crofting communities.

The A87 south runs along Glen Varragill with the Cuillin soon coming into view as the road makes its pleasant and short journey to the junction with the A863 at Sligachan.

3. South to Skye Bridge and Raasay

Kyleakin and Skye Bridge

As the route is retraced from Sligachan the road leads again to Broadford

with all its amenities and services. Ahead the A87 winds through the settlement bordering central Broadford until it opens out en-route to the bridge. Just three miles from Broadford a minor road to the right is signposted to **Kylerhea** and to the ferry (summer only). This is one of the more tortuous minor roads following the river and winding above Glen Arroch. There are few buildings along this route nor are there too many passing places so,

with a number of blind summits, care is required in negotiating this road. Just as the tiny township of Kylerhea comes into view and before the road drops sharply to the shore is the track leading to the Forestry Commission Otter hide.

Turning left here leads to a car park and from there a broad path can be taken with superb views over the Sound of Sleat across to Glenelg on the main road. This is an area which

abounds with wildlife and therefore, dogs are not allowed on this trail. As you leave the car park and pass through the gate the visitor is on the nature reserve. Otters are a protected species so to knowingly disturb them is an offence and nor should their bolt be approached. This is a very pleasant place to wander even if you are not lucky enough to spot the otters which frequent the waters of the sound.

The Kylerhea narrows have been a natural choice for crossing by sea from Skye to the mainland for centuries. It is the shortest distance, just 550 metres from Kylerhea to **Glenelg**, itself a place worthy of visiting. For years the drovers crossed their cattle by this route and there was a ferry here as long ago as the late 1600s. Until railways were built leading to Mallaig and Kyle of Lochalsh on the mainland this was an important route to Skye. A car ferry ran from 1934 until the 1950s when the lack of traffic following the war meant it was discontinued. If the visitor is looking for a different, and interesting route from Skye, then the summer ferry service is a good choice.

A ferry service was reinstigated in 1959 and by the seventies there were two car ferries. Again threatened with closure in 2005, the ferry service was saved by a group of local people, from both sides of the narrows, forming a community interest company and

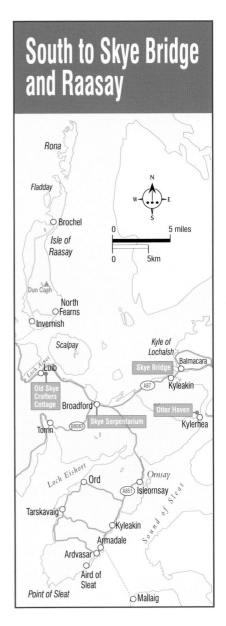

South to Skye Bridge and Raasay

raising the necessary funds to buy a vessel, the *Glenachulish* in 2006. She is the last of the traditional manually operated turntable ferries which were once a common feature of the highlands and islands. The crossing, although short, can be a revelation in terms of wildlife spotting. Pods of porpoise, bottle nose dolphins and minke whales are frequently seen and occasionally the Orca, the killer whale. Otters and seals complement the diversity of wildlife.

Many birds are also spotted including oyster-catchers, razorbills, arctic terns and cormorants. Sometimes gannets and puffins make an appearance. On the mainland side Glenelg Bay is an area where kittiwakes gather prior to breeding.

If the ferry is not taken (no need to book, just turn up and wait in turn) then the return to the A87 is by the same road and then a right turn arriving very quickly at the only roundabout on Skye, at the foot of the Skye bridge.

Before crossing the bridge, straight over the roundabout lies Kyleakin, once very busy with the ferry service from Kyle of Lochalsh making frequent summer trips from the mainland. Kyleakin was, for a long time the gateway to Skye. The ferry service here was in existence from at least 1841 and summer visitors in those days really did have to go 'over the sea to Skye'. Whether some romance has disappeared with the building of the bridge is a matter of debate although the author would contend that Skye has enough romance, mystery, legend and splendour to hold her own whatever method of travel brings visitors to her shores.

Skye Bridge

Skye bridge opened in 1995 and the very same day the ferries ceased leaving an expensive, and controversial, toll bridge in their place. Controversy raged over the excessive tolls being charged and, eventually, public opinion held sway. Finally in December 2004 the tolls were abolished and the bridge is now free to vehicles from either direction.

Since the bridge was built Kyleakin has become much quieter than it used to be when the plentiful accommodation and restaurants were full to overflowing during the summer months. It deserves not to be bypassed by visitors hurrying north. For one thing it still has enough amenities to serve the visitors, some excellent hotels and from the bay, an excellent view of the bridge and lighthouse.

It is also home to the Bright Water Visitor Centre which is highly recommended. From the Centre tours run to the island of Eilean Ban, a wildlife haven under the new bridge. Otters frequent these waters and inspired the author Gavin Maxwell, who owned Eilean Ban and wrote *Ring of Bright Water*. The island is a commemorative otter sanctuary and partly funded by the Born Free Foundation.

Kyleakin has a redesigned and pleasant central harbour from where four short walks set out and makes a good resting and meeting place. Kyleakin also has four pubs where you can enjoy a Skye welcome.

From the harbour the routes of four walks are marked and these take the visitor, repectively, to Castle Maol, along the Salt Marsh to spot wildlife, along the seafront and to the war memorial from where you can watch ships passing with panoramic views as a backdrop.

Nearby on a rocky promontory, are the ruins of **Castle Maol** or Castle Moil as it is often known. This ancient fortress was once known as Dunakin, and prior to that Dun Haakon, and dates back over one thousand years.

Once the home of a Norwegian princess nicknamed 'Saucy Mary' Dunakin commanded the narrow sound between Skye and the mainland. Cashing in on its ideal position, it is said that Saucy Mary and her husband, the fourth MacKinnon chief, ran a heavy chain across the sound and charged all passing ships a toll for use of the seaway. Those that did not pay would have to attempt the stormier waters of the Minch.

As the visitor passes over the bridge it is worth reflecting how easy our passage is made in modern times but how little, in many respects, Skye has changed. For most people Skye is a place that stays with them and inevitably, calls them back to enjoy its history, dramatic landscape, quiet calm corners, incredible sunsets and night skies and a range of wildlife unlikely to be seen in any other part of Britain.

Raasay

With its small population, around 200, and, effectively, one road with a spur east to North Fearns, Raasay remains one of the loveliest and most unspoilt of islands. The roads is does have hardly

qualify as main roads and there is no petrol station on the island so it is worth remembering to refuel at Broadford the nearest of petrol stations on Skye.

What Raasay is though, is superb walking country and a natural home to an abundance of wildlife, flowers and plants that bring a riot of colour to the island. In summer the ferry from Sconser makes nine crossings a day, augmented by the boat from Raasay House transporting more visitors.

Raasay's people were cleared by the landlord to make way for sheep which, with red deer roam amongst the deserted villages abandoned in the 1800s. Nowadays, almost all the population live in the south near the village of Inverarish and close to the ferry route from Skye.

The moorlands, sea cliffs and forests of the island support sixty species of birds amongst which are grouse, kestrels, buzzards and golden eagles. Wading birds can be heard in the summer around the bays and inlets dotted around the island.

For the most part Raasay is as wild and unspoilt as the visitor could wish, and a delight for walkers. As the island is approached it is easy to spot the old railway which runs from the pier (where a foundry once flourished but now lies in ruins) to the old iron ore mine at the edge of the forest. This mine was once worked by German prisoners during the first world war; today picnic tables are provided by the car park.

To walk to the old mine step over the fence by the ferry waiting room from where you can reach the track. Follow the old railway as it heads straight uphill and through part of the forest until the line emerges onto a single track road by a car park. The entrance to the mine is just behind an old ruined building. This simple walk is about three miles there and back and, if you do not have a car, the village of Inverarish can be reached from the single track road quite quickly instead of returning to the start.

The highest point on the island, **Dun Caan**, has a distinctive flat top and gives superb views from its 1,100ft top. It calls to be climbed and the starting point is the end of the railway line, by the old mine.

Although not difficult, the route to Dun Caan requires some care mainly due to the path becoming indistinct in places. Initially follow the signs for the Burma Road Trail, through a gate and over the bridge. At a second bridge Dun Caan is signposted so take the steep footpath beside Inverarish burn and over a stile onto the hillside. As the path rises out of the glen Dun Caan itself comes into view. The path is unclear as you reach a cairn but just head for the second cairn slightly left and ahead. After reaching this within a few yards the path improves, running alongside the loch and by the boulders at the head of the loch. From here the route turns uphill, crosses another path and zigzags up to the summit of Dun Caan. Stay awhile and enjoy the panoramic views before returning by the same route. The distance there and back is about six miles.

There is a choice of accommodation in and around Inverarish from the youth hostel to the hotel with a guest house, bed and breakfast and the Raasay Outdoor Centre at Raasay House where there is café/bar, restaurant,

shop and visitor centre. A wide range of activities are on offer here so it is an ideal place for children. Many lovely walks are possible from Inverarish, from Raasay House and around the forest. In the evening a saunter down to the old pier to watch the sun go down over the Skye mountains across the water is a perfect end to a day.

From Inverarish one road leads east, past the old mine to the village of North Fearns. The cottages here have been restored and this is where the road ends on the south eastern side of the island.

Please park carefully here at the car park allowing space for other vehicles. From **North Fearns** follow the wide grassy track which takes you to the deserted cleared village of Hallaig, It is about an hours walk on a good path and from here the shore is easily accessible; there is also a waterfall nearby. This peaceful spot is evocative of those terrible times in highland history when crofters where cruelly treated by landowners, resulting in so many deserted villages around the highlands.

The east coast can, in fact, be walked from North Fearns to **Screapadal** and thence to rejoin the road north or return the same route. Past Hallaig the route is quite strenuous and the way

Left: The Raasay Ferry approaching Sconsor on Loch Sligachan

Opposite: The Red Cuillin from Raasay

Below: Raasay and South Rona Island to the left across the Sound of Raasay

quite slow so do be prepared if you decide to attempt the entire route.

Rejoining the Inverarish road you head north along a road which runs almost parallel to the coast. At times it affords excellent views in some places. The car park by Loch Eader is the start of another route towards Dun Caan summit. Just a little further on limited space for parking at Glame Brae allows for a visit to Inver Bay.

Parking carefully here at the bottom of Glame Brae (a brae is a hill) and take the clear path to Inver. The route takes you through birch woods following the river and leads to Inver Bay which is a sandy bay where eider ducks are known to nest. This short walk takes little more than an hour and is a lovely simple walk to a beautiful bay and well worth taking.

From this point the road takes the visitor to Brochel Castle, now in ruins and this is where the road originally ended. Now, it is the start of Calum's road which has become a symbol of one man's single-minded determination. As described in the introduction, Calum MacLeod built this road over the course of ten years hard work and you can honour his memory by driving the short distance from Brochel to Arnish where Calum lived and died.

From Arnish the way north can be explored, but on foot. Since many visitors fail to leave their cars and explore further this remains a totally unspoilt area with great views at various points along the way and a walk out to **Fladda Island**.

First, you need to walk through the birch woods to Torran on a clear path. This is a pleasant 20 minute stroll. From Torran the path bears left, remaining clear, and in another 30 minutes you reach the shoreline at the bay with Fladda island only just offshore; the island is, however, cut off at high tide so always check tide times before setting out. If you are caught on the island there is no choice but to wait for the next low tide unless, of course, you prefer to swim. The bay here is full of mussels and some of them contain the smallest of pearls. It is also an ideal vantage point to look across to Skye with the Storr and the Quiraing easily recognisable.

From Fladda a further route takes you all the way to Kyle Rona, just across the waters from Rona island. It takes almost two hours to continue to the point passing the ruined township of **Umachan**. Along the way it is possible to see the Torridon hills on the mainland and Staffin headland on Skye. For peace and tranquillity and beautiful surroundings this part of Raasay is unmissable.

Raasay is one of those special places that has escaped so much of twentieth century life yet still offers all the amenities visitors expect. The islanders are a close knit community who care very much for their special island; visitors are very welcome and given true highland hospitality but please do respect this island and help to protect the environment and wildlife. It is also expected that dogs will be kept on a lead at all times.

Taken together, Skye and Raasay offer time out that leaves you with very precious memories; there is no reason to rush and every reason to take time and allow yourself to fall in love with Skye and Raasay, they will reward your appreciation a thousandfold.

Places to Visit

South – Garden of Skye

Armadale Castle, Gardens & Museum of the Isles
Armadale, IV45 8RS
☎ 01471 844305
www.clandonald.com
Open: Apr-Oct, 9.30am-5.30pm, daily

Skye Serpentarium
The Old Mill
Broadford, IV49 9AQ
☎ 01471 822209
www.skyeserpentarium.org.uk

Talisker Distillery
Carbost
☎ 01478 614308
www.discovering-distilleries.com
Open: Easter-Oct, 9.30am-5pm, Mon-Sat;
Jul-Aug, also Sun, 12.30pm-5pm;
Nov-Mar, Mon-Fri by appt. only
Closed Christmas and New Year. Last tour
one hour before closing.
Note: there is a charge for admission,
redeemable in the distillery shop.

North

Aros (Visitor Centre)
Viewfield Road, Portree
☎ 01478 613649
www.aros.co.uk
Award winning visitor experience

Colbost Croft Museum
4 miles from Dunvegan on the Glendale
road.
☎ 01470 521296
Open: Easter-end Sept, 10am-6.30pm,
daily

Dunvegan Castle
☎ 01470 521206
www.dunvegancastle.com
Open: Easter-end-October, 10am-
5.30pmp; Nov-Mar 11am-4pm
Skye's premier attraction. Home of the
Chiefs of MacLeod

Giant Angus MacAskill Museum
Main street Dunvegan
☎ 01470 521296
Open: 9.30am-6.30pm, daily

Glendale Toy Museum
☎ 01470 511240
www.toy-museum.co.uk
Open: 10am-6pm, Mon-Sat

Isle of Skye Soap Co
Somerled Square
Portree, IV51 9EH
☎ 01478 611350
Handcrafted aromatherapy soaps and
oils

Shilasdair
Waternish
☎ 01470 592297
The Skye Yarn Company making woollen
sweaters

Skyeskyns
Stein
Waternish, IV55 8GD
☎ 01470 592237
www.skyeskyns.co.uk
Open: 9am-6pm, daily
Exhibition tannery, free guided tour

Staffin Dinosaur Museum
☎ 01470 562302
Open: Easter-end of summer 10.30am-
1pm, Mon, Tue, Thur, Fri, (telephone in
advance)

The Skye Ferry departs from Mallaig

Road signs are bilingual: English and Gaelic

FACTFILE: ISLE OF SKYE

Travelling to Skye

Skye is easy to reach by car, ferry or public transport. There are rail links to Kyle of Lochalsh from Inverness and to Mallaig from Glasgow. CityLink buses run from Inverness, Edinburgh and Glasgow directly to Portree, the island capital. The Caledonian MacBrayne ferry from Mallaig serves Armadale and the community ferry operates from Glenelg on the mainland to Kylerhea. Both ferries carry vehicles and passengers.

By car visitors can use the Skye Bridge without toll charge arriving at Kyleakin.

Scotrail

National rail enquiries ☎ 08457 48 49 50
Telesales bookings ☎ 08457 55 00 33

CityLink Buses

Enquiry / booking line ☎ 08705 50 50 50
Calmac Ferries
Enquiries and reservations ☎ 08705 65 00 00

Inverness Airport

www.invernessairport.com/airlinees for details of airlines from various regions operating to and from Inverness.

Glenelg Community Ferry

No telephone booking service but ferries run every 20 minutes during summer (May to end-Sep) from 9am-7pm Mon-Sat; (from the last Sunday in May) 10am-6pm Sundays. Always check with Tourist Office for current service.

West Highland Flyer

☎ 07780 72 42 48
Oban to Mallaig leaves Oban at 9.45am arriving Mallaig 12.15pm. Mallaig to Oban leaves Mallaig 6.00pm arriving Oban 8.30pm. Summer service only Monday to Saturday.

Getting around Skye

Skye still has a number of single-track roads and care should be taken using these. Passing places are provided to give way to oncoming traffic and should also be used to allow overtaking. Local residents are accustomed to these roads and often wish to overtake and appreciate being allowed to do so. Be watchful for sheep straying onto the roads as accidents are not uncommon. If an animal is injured please report the incident to the local police.

Public Transport

Rapsons Buses (part of Highland Country buses)

☎ 01463 710555
All routes start and end at Portree. Timetables available from Tourist Information Centres in Portree, Dunvegan and Broadford. Be aware that some services only operate during school term times.

Skye Flyer

☎ 07780 72 42 48
Connects with the 1.35pm ferry from Mallaig, leaves Armadale Terminal at 2.10pm via Broadford, Sconser and Portree to arrive Uig ferry terminal 3.30pm.
Return journey leaves Uig terminal 3.30pm and arrives Armadale 4.50pm.

Postbus

Operates from Dunvegan post office; this service carries up to four passengers and serves the Glendale area. Check with post office for departure times.

Sconser – Raasay Ferry
Operated by Caledonian MacBrayne ☎ 08705 65 00 00

Car Hire on Skye

Portree Coachworks
Portree Industrial Estate
Portree
☎ 01478 612688

Ewen MacCrae
Dunvegan Road
Portree
☎ 01478 612554

Jansvans
Portree Industrial Estate
Portree
☎ 01478 612087

Sutherland Garage
Main A87
Broadford
☎ 01471 822225

Cycle Hire

Fairwinds Cycles
Elgol Road
Broadford
☎ 01470 822270

Island Cycles
The Green
Portree
☎ 01478 613121

Taxis

Dunvegan Taxis
☎ 01470 521560

Ace Taxis
☎ 01478 613456

Garages and breakdown

Ewen MacRae
Dunvegan Road, Portree
☎ 01478 612554

Sutherland Garage
Main A87, Broadford
☎ 01471 822225

KennysGarage
Lonmore, Dunvegan
☎ 01470 521648

Accommodation

Skye has a wide range of hotels, guest houses, bed and breakfasts and self-catering accommodation many with glorious views and ranging from budget to 5 star luxury.

Visitscotland
National accommodation and bookings ☎ 0845 22 55 121

Self-catering
www.visitscotland.com
www.islandsandhighlandscottages.co.uk

Bunkhouses and hostels
www.hostel-scotland.co.uk
www.syha.org.uk

Booking Bureaux available throught Tourist Information Centres:
Bayfield House, Bayfield Road, Portree ☎ 01478 614906
2 Lochside, Dunvegan ☎ 01470 521581
Car Park, Broadford ☎ 01471 822713

Camping and Caravan Sites

Torvaig Caravan & Camping
Portree
☎ 01478 611849

Glenbrittle Campsite
MacLeod Estate Office
☎ 01478 640404

Loch Greshornish
Edinbane
☎ 01470 582230

Uig Campsite
Uig
☎ 01470 542714

Banks

Bank of Scotland
Somerled Square
Portree
☎ 01478 612438

Broadford Bay
Broadford
☎ 01471 822457

Churches

Baptist

Broadford

Roman Catholic

Portree and Broadford

Church of Scotland

At: Kyleakin, Broadford, Kilmore, Dunvegan, Portree, Uig, Carbost and Kensaleyre.
Free Presbyterian Church of Scotland
At: Carbost, Portnalong, Dunvegan, Glendale, Waternish, Kilmuir, Staffin, Uig, Teangue (Sleat), Kyleakin, Portree and Inverarish, Isle of Raasay.

Scottish Episcopal

St Columba's, off Somerled Square, Portree
St Michael's, Isle of Raasay

Doctors' Surgeries

Sleat Medical Practice
Teangue, IV44 8RQ
☎ 01471 844283

Carbost Medical Practice
Carbost, IV47 8SR
☎ 01478 640202

Broadford Medical Centre
High Road, Broadford, IV49 9AA
☎ 01471 822460

Dunvegan Medical Centre
Dunvegan
Dunvegan, IV55 8GU

Portree Medical Centre
Fairy Hill, Portree, IV51 9BZ
☎ 01478 612013

Emergency Numbers

Police ☎ 999

Fire ☎ 999

Police stations at Broadford, Dunvegan, Portree and Uig.
Main Portree station ☎ 01478 612888

Lifeboat
The Pier, Portree, IV51 9DD ☎ 01478 613610

Mountain Rescue
Main bases at Sligachan and Glenbrittle. Permanent dog team based on the island. Contact ☎ 01478 612888

Veterinary Surgeons
Bernisdale
☎ 01470 532385
Broadford
☎ 01471 822922
Portree (Snizort)
☎ 01470 532278

Festivals and Events

Skye Highland Games
The Lump, Portree
August

Feis an Eilein – The Skye Festival
Sleat, South Skye
July

Skye Scene Highland Ceilidh
Portree every Tues and Wed from end-May to end-August

Isle of Skye Accordian & Fiddle Festival
May

Armadale Castle Garden Fair
May

Dunvegan Gala Day
May

Quaich Piping Competition
Armadale Castle
June

Skye Pipe Band Festival
Portree
July

Skye Agricultural Show
August

Blas Festival
September

Skye & Lochalsh Arts & Crafts Show
July
☎ 01478 612697

Glendale & NW Skye Crafts Fair
August

Local Produce

Seafood

Anchor Seafoods
The Pier, Portree
☎ 01478 612414

*Isle of Skye Oysters
Beach View, Fiskavag
☎ 01478 640313

Isle of Skye Seafood
Industrial Estate, Broadford
☎ 01471 822135

*Loch Bracadale Crabs
Eabost, Struan
☎ 01470 572264

*Loch Dunvegan Mussels
Kilmuir, Dunvegan
☎ 01470 521394

*Oakes Marine
Sconser
☎ 01478 650304

Potty Preserves
Glendale
☎ 01470 511343
* Please telephone prior to arrival.

Sweet Things

Claire Macdonald Luxury Comestibles
Kinloch Lodge, Sleat
01471 833214

Isle of Skye Fudge
Dunvegan
please contact by email
info@skyefudge.co.uk

Vanilla Skye (chocolates)
Portree
☎ 01478 611295

Shops

Alba FarmShop
Upper Breakish, Broadford
☎ 01471 520000

Fasgadh Stores
Dunvegan
☎ 01470 521432

Fruit and Nut Place
Dunvegan
☎ 01470 521480

Fruit and Nut Place
Struan

Sleat Trading
Armadale Pier
☎ 01471 844265

Jacksons Wholefoods
Portree
☎ 01478 613326

Whisky

Talisker Distillery
Colbost
☎ 01478 614300

Brewery

Isle of Skye Brewing Co.,
The Pier, Uig
☎ 01470 542477

OS Maps

OS Landranger series nos 23, 32, 33 and 39
OS Explorer series nos 407, 408, 409, 410, 411 and 412

Post Offices

Broadford
☎ 01471 822201

Carbost Village
☎ 01478 640286

Dunvegan
☎ 01470 521201

Portree
☎ 01478 612533

Recommended Reading

Dempster, Andrew	Skye 360	Luath Press
Hutchinson, Roger	Calum's Road	Birlinn
Swire, Otta	Skye, The Island and its Legends	Birlinn
MacDonald, J	Discovering Skye	J MacDonald
Cooper, Derek	Skye	Birlinn
Yoxon, P & G	Prehistoric Skye	Skye Environmental Centre
Nicolson, A	History of Skye	MacLean Press

Restaurants

Skye has a range of top quality restaurants in all areas and here I am highlighting those which I have found to be excellent, using local produce and therefore recommended.

South Skye

Eileann Iarmain Hotel
Isle Ornsay
☎ 01471 833332

Toravaig House Hotel
Sleat
☎ 01471 820200

Kinloch Lodge Hotel
nr Broadford
☎ 01471 833333

Creelers
Broadford
☎ 01471 822281

The Broadford Hotel
Broadford
☎ 01471 822204

MacKinnon Country House Hotel
Kyleakin
☎ 01599 534180

The Pasta Shed
Armadale Pier
☎ 01471 844222

North Skye

The Three Chimneys
Colbost
☎ 01470 511258

The Old School Restaurant
Dunvegan
☎ 01470 521421

The Stein Inn
Stein
☎ 01470 592362

Ullinish Country Lodge Hotel
nr Struan
☎ 01470 572214

Loch Bay Seafood Restaurant
☎ 01470 592235

Marmalade
Portree
☎ 01478 611711

Café Arriba
Portree
☎ 01478 611830

Sea Breezes
Portree
☎ 01478 612016

Chandlery Restaurant
Portree
☎ 01478 612846

Greshornish House Hotel
nr Edinbane
☎ 01470 582266

Sport and Outdoor Adventure

Boat Cruises and Wildlife Watching

Portree Area

MV Stardust
☎ 07798 743858**

Elgol Area

Bella Jane Cruises and Aquaxplore
☎ 0800 731 3089

Misty Isle Boats
☎ 01471 866288

Dunvegan Area

Seal-watching Trips, Macleod Estate, Dunvegan
Castle
☎ 01470 521206

South Skye

Sea.fari Adventures
Armadale Pier
☎ 01471 833316
**Other operators offer boat trips from Portree
harbour but at the time of going to press
websites were not operating and there were no
telephone contact numbers available.

Fishing

North Skye

Skeabost House Hotel
(River Snizort)
☎ 01470 532202

Jansport
Portree
(Storr Lochs)
☎ 01478 612559

Central Skye

Campsite Shop
Glenbrittle
(River Brittle)
☎ 01478 640404

South Skye

Sligachan Hotel
(River Sligachan)
☎ 01478 650204

Estate Office
Eilean Iarmain, Sleat
(Loch na Dubhraichean, Loch Barabhaig, Loch Lonachan, Loch Iasgaich)
☎ 01471 833266
Permits available from the above. Contact local Tourist Information Centre for any private ghillie service which may operate. Tourist Information also has a useful leaflet detailing permit-free fishing access on Skye

General and Wildlife Tours

Red Deer Travel
Portree

Skye WildTours
Shona Mackenzie
Skeabost Bridge

Isle of Skye Tour Guide Company
Kilmore
Sleat

Wildlife Tours
Rob Lawson
Torrin

Skye in Focus
Ard Dorch
On the Wing, Aros Centre, Portree
Tourist Information Centres have full details

Golf

Isle of Skye Golf Club
Sconser
☎ 01478 650414

Skeabost Golf Club
Skeabost nr Portree
☎ 01470 532202

Both are 9-hole courses

Mountain Guide Services

Blaven Guiding
☎ 01478 613180

Skye Guides
☎ 01471 822116

Hebridean Pathways
☎ 07092 840603

Climb Skye
☎ 01478 640264

Skye Mountain Guides
☎ 01478 612682

Guiding on Skye
☎ 01478 650380

Outdoor / Adventure Sports

Whitewaves
Kilmuir, Trotternish
☎ 01470 542414

Dive and Sea the Hebrides
Stein
Waternish
☎ 01470 592219

Skyakadventures
Isle Ornsay South Skye
☎ 01471 833428
Also at Broadford Pier – range of watersports and boating activities

Isle of Skye Yachts
Armadale Pier
yacht charter available
Staffin Bay Cruises
☎ 01470 562217

89

White tailed Sea Eagles

This magnificent bird, Britain's largest and rarest bird of prey, was persecuted to the point of extinction by 1930. It was through a reintroduction programme begun in 1968 in Fair Isle that their presence in Scotland was established and, after being introduced to Rum in 1975 they found their way to Skye. The present day population is around 30 breeding pairs mostly on the islands of Skye and Rum. Breeding sites are protected and the RSPB (Royal Society for the Protection of Birds) and SNH (Scottish Natural Heritage) work together in monitoring and managing the project. They could be seen on almost any of the routes on Skye in this book and are, once seen and recognised, quite easy to identify. Apart from their size, they are recognisable by their brown body and much paler head and neck with the distinctive white tail feathers.

Sea eagles pair for life and on average will live for 21 years. Nesting sites are not disclosed because, unfortunately, there are still those who would steal their eggs; prizing the collection of eggs above the lives of these remarkable birds.

Although many visitors hope to see these eagles it is worth bearing in mind the disturbance that man causes; the site near Portree has failed and a contributory factor is that the boat trips run from the harbour visit this area right from the start of the breeding season. Boats have been seen going far too close to the nest site. In addition, there is a practise amongst some operators to throw fish from the boat to allow visitors to see the sea eagles catching the fish. This alone means an unnatural imbalance is established which is not helpful to the birds. Moreover a recent and controversial practice is that of putting cork or polystyrene into the fish to make them float so that visitors have a better view. Gulls or other birds swallowing fish with cork or polystyrene, which has been seen happening, will die. This is a very irresponsible practice and Scottish Natural Heritage are hoping that a code of practice can be introduced which can allow visitors to enjoy the birdlife without endangering the lives of birds who live by their catch from the sea.

When visiting, please ensure that you help protect our wildlife by taking boat trips with operators who do not engage in practices which cause disturbance, distress or death to our wild creatures. It may be worth noting that the operators who run the boat trips from Elgol work ethically and, at the time of writing, do not engage in these practices.

Riding/Pony Trekking

Cuillin Trail Riding
Struan
☎ 01470 572324

Skye Beaches for Children

Coral Beach
Dunvegan
unique coral bay. Dogs may be prohibited when livestock are present. Walk from car park to beach approximately 1 mile.

Fiscavaig Bay
Lovely wide bay with rock pools and best razor fish collecting on Skye. Very fast tide.

Glenbrittle Beach
Best known wide sandy beach with parking and shop. Nearby campsite. Views to the Small Isles.

Staffin Bay
Great sandy beach when the tide is out. Good beach-cast fishing.
Camus Mhor Bay

Braes
Little known and an ideal activity trip for children. Two bays with caves to explore. Approximately _ mile walk from Balmeanach

Talisker Bay
Park carefully and walk about 1 mile to lovely bay and view across to impressive waterfall. Livestock may be present.

Elgol Bay
Very stony beach with fabulous views towards the Cuillin.

Tourist Information Centres

Bayfield House, Bayfield Road, Portree ☎ 01478 614906
2 Lochside, Dunvegan ☎ 01470 521581
Car Park, Broadford ☎ 01471 822713

Wet weather attractions

Clan Donald Visitor Centre and Armadale Castle (w)
Museum of the Isles (w)
Bright Water Visitor Centre (w)
Aros Centre (w)
Serpentarium and Reptile World (w)
Talisker Distillery (w)
Museum of Island Life (w)
Isle of Skye Brewery (w)
Skye Silver (w)
Glendale Toy Museum (w)
Borreraig Park, Piping Centre and Museum (w)
Dunvegan Castle (w)
Otter Hide, Kylerhea
Colbost Croft Museum (w)
Skyeskins (w)
In addition, Skye boasts a host of studios and galleries displaying the range of talented artists and craftspeople based on Skye. The free booklet *Elements of Excellence* lists all members of the Skye

and Lochalsh Arts and Crafts Association and is widely available including from Tourist Information Centres. The listings are arranged in geographical groupings giving a number of 'studio trails' for the visitor taking in a variety of studios and galleries.

Always check current opening times with Tourist Information Centres as published opening times may well not apply.

Websites

www.skye.co.uk	a guide to all things Skye
www.skyewalk.co.uk	excellent site with numerous walks on Skye
www.craftsonskye.org.uk	NW Skye crafts and art
www.slaca.co.uk	Skye and Lochalsh crafts website

FACTFILE: ISLE OF RAASAY

This island, a little gem just off the coast of Skye, is easy to reach via the CalMac ferry service from Sconser (passenger and vehicle ferry) and rewards a visit. Most of the population live around Inverarish and this is where the General Store and Post Office (☎ 01478 660203) is to be found.

Accommodation

Isle of Raasay Hotel & restaurant
☎ 01478 660222

Raasay House & Outdoor Centre
Clachan, Raasay
☎ 01478 660266
Offers instruction in sailing, rock climbing, abseiling, kayaking, canoeing and outdoor education. Now operating out of the Borodale Hotel during the rebuilt following a major fire in January 2009.

Churchton Guest House
☎ 01478 660260

Allt Arais bed and breakfast
☎ 01478 660237

Youth Hostel
☎ 0870 004 1146

Responsible camping, although no official sites exist, is permitted on the island.

Activities

Raasay Outdoor Centre offers a range of activities including sailing, windsurfing, climbing, abseiling and canoeing. Evening activities and events for the family in the extensive grounds are also arranged throughout the season.

Shooting (autumn only)
Fishing
Cycling
Walking – numerous routes including the famous Calum's Road and the route to Dun Caan
Boat trip to Rona, Raasay's tiny neighbour. Or contact Rona's caretaker, Bill Cowie for information on accommodation and trips from Rona itself. Email ronalodge@tiscali.co.uk or telephone 07831 293963.

Places to visit

Calum's Road
Brochel Castle
Raasay Museum
Hallaig lost township
Dun Caan (highest peak)
St Moluag's Chapel

Events

The Raasay Rumble, a 10-hour mountain bike race each September.

Index

Index